THE
EDWARDIAN
HOUSE
EXPLAINED

THE
EDWARDIAN
HOUSE
EXPLAINED

── TREVOR YORKE ──

COUNTRYSIDE BOOKS
NEWBURY BERKSHIRE

Contents

Introduction

What do we imagine when asked to describe an Edwardian house? Some may think of a country mansion catering for endless weekend parties, the backdrop to yet another period murder mystery! To others it might be a suburban semi-detached house, a large, stout building embodying all that was good about the final years of the Victorian world before the outbreak of war. To most it conjures up images of red brick structures with grey slate or tiled roofs, stained glass patterns in the tops of windows, white painted balconies and surrounded by spacious lawns, a house suited to the lazy summers that this proud, imperial nation seemed to enjoy in the opening decade of the 20th century.

Yet there is far more to the Edwardian period than first meets the eye. It was a time of great social contrasts, fears of technology and all things foreign, and shifts in political power. For many there was greater freedom, a higher standard of living and better housing while others were still struggling in squalid accommodation, poorly paid jobs with dangerous conditions and long hours, and with the threat of unemployment hanging over them. Some sought security in the past and the glorification of the British Empire while others looked forward to social reform and development in working practices. This period should be seen as both the Indian summer of the Victorian world and the awakening of a modern and vibrant new century.

These contrasts are evident in the housing of the time, which, far from falling neatly into a type, consists of a wide mixture of sizes, styles and layouts. You will find new, inventive plans but with olde worlde façades, 18th century style classical houses yet fitted with the latest in technology, and spacious, light and airy Arts and Crafts buildings only a short distance from tightly packed, dark and dingy terraces. There were some that would still be fashionable in the 1930s and others that went out of vogue in the 1880s!

For those of us who live in an Edwardian house or are interested in the subject, trying to unravel this vast range of house types, recognise the various styles, establish how they originally appeared and work out who was likely to have lived in them can be challenging. Architectural writers on the subject can be rather dismissive of the mass housing of this period, while others immerse themselves in describing fashionable details that were only enjoyed by a select few. This book is intended as an easy-to-understand guide for people making their first step into this subject and wanting to find out more about the houses, large and small, grand or plain, which we are likely to live in or see today. It will provide readers with a fascinating background knowledge of all aspects of Edwardian housing, whether they are renovating, tracing the history of their own house or simply wanting to know more about this notable period in history.

The book is divided into three sections. The first outlines the story of the Edwardian Age and how housing developed, with drawings and photos to illustrate the different layouts, styles and exterior details. The second section steps inside the house and looks at the various rooms and their fittings, what they were used for and how they may have originally appeared. The final part includes details of places to visit, a glossary explaining some of the terms used and brief notes to help you date your house.

Trevor Yorke

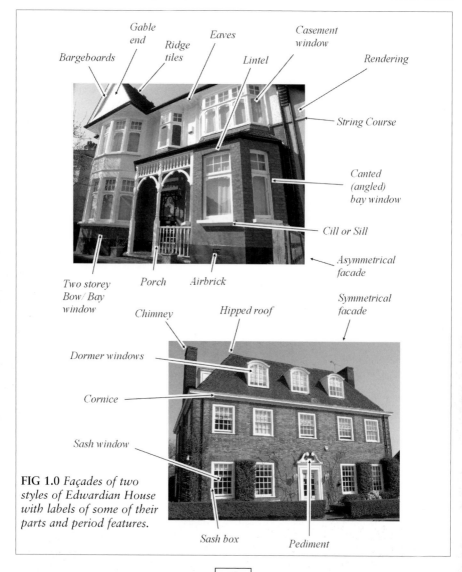

FIG 1.0 *Façades of two styles of Edwardian House with labels of some of their parts and period features.*

SECTION I

THE EDWARDIAN AGE AND ITS HOUSING

CHAPTER I

Edwardian Times
Contrast and Tradition

FIG 1.1: SION HILL HALL, THIRSK, YORKSHIRE: *One of the last great houses, built just before the First World War by Walter H. Brierley, often referred to as the 'Lutyens of the North'. The steep pitched roof with overhanging eaves, prominent but plain chimneys and the symmetrical façade were inspired by late 17th and early 18th century houses, but were arranged in new forms by both architects.*

L iterature, films and photographs of the Edwardian period give us today a vision in sepia of a long lost imperial world resplendent in pomp and ceremony, with poignant images of weekend parties and lazy days by the river all set in a seemingly endless summer. It appears from this distance that it represented the final flowering of the British Empire, a confident time celebrated in magnificent buildings and rousing anthems, led by ambitious men and world leading innovators, with a population that spent a large proportion

creating the foundations for the 20th century. And in reality the summers were not that good either!

The Fall of the Landed Classes

The accession to the throne of the notorious and disreputable Prince of Wales in 1901 played its part in welcoming in a lighter, more relaxed attitude to life especially among the younger generation. Gone was the distant and austere Queen; now there was a new King whose fashionable, lavish and extravagant lifestyle fulfilled the public's image of an imperial monarch and fuelled a fascination with the aristocracy. The super-rich seemed to be on an endless cycle of long weekend parties, great shoots and gambling, their year based around the London Season from spring to

FIG 1.2: STOCKPORT TOWN HALL, GREATER MANCHESTER: *For major Edwardian public buildings there was a rejection of the red brick Gothic that had been popular in the mid to late Victorian period and a return to classical architecture, in this case the flamboyant Baroque of the late 17th and early 18th centuries (see Fig 1.5).*

of their earnings on hats. In reality, however, it was a period of anxiety with the realisation that all was not well with our colonial acquisitions, the economy and the conditions and social status of too many of its inhabitants. It was a time of great contrasts not only between rich and poor but also between the embracing of inventions and the obsession with preserving the past. Far from being a decadent, leisurely decade it was one in which ground breaking new legislation and political ideas were laid down,

FIG 1.3: SANDRINGHAM PALACE, NORFOLK: *Purchased in 1862 by the Prince of Wales, later King Edward VII, as a country estate for shooting parties and entertaining, it was largely rebuilt a few years later (the left-hand part in this view) and extended in 1892 (the right-hand side). This sociable monarch, although popular with the working classes, was seen as disreputable by the more serious minded middle classes and it was only his role of country gentleman on his Sandringham estate that gained their favour.*

summer, then sailing at Cowes or off to the French Riviera before returning for the Glorious 12th and the Hunt (during a three-day shoot at Sandringham in 1905, we are told that the King and his guests managed to shoot down more than 6,000 birds).

However, not all gentlemen were able to enjoy this lifestyle, especially those whose wealth had been dependent upon rents from their estates, money that dried up as a result of the halving of land values in the wake of the agricultural depression of the late 1800s. These difficulties were intensified by the King's own government, which from the late 19th century was elected by an increased proportion of the population, loosening the landed gentry's traditional grip on power (Asquith who became Prime Minister in 1908 was the first to do so without a country seat). With the introduction of – and subsequent increases in – taxes on the super rich and their property, including death duties, many were forced into cutbacks, selling their town residences and retreating to the country, or at worst losing their seat completely. More than fifty great houses were demolished or abandoned in this period. There was, however, plenty of new money floating around, ready to snap up a bargain title, house and estate. As the effects of the slump in farming and the 'boom and bust' nature in elements of the economy were patchy, there were some who did well in this period – especially those in finance, who were ready to buy into the aristocratic image.

The Liberal government that came to power in 1906 intended to use much of the revenue from taxing the rich to pay for new social policies. Although the welfare state is associated with the post Second World War period, the first pensions and national insurance schemes

FIG 1.4: CASTLE DROGO, DEVON: *Regarded as the last major country house built in England. It was designed by Sir Edwin Lutyens for Julius Drewe, the founder of the Home and Colonial Stores, in 1910–11 but was not completed until 1930 and then on a reduced scale.*

were actually introduced by Lloyd George in his 1909 budget. An after effect of this, however, was the Parliament Act, which was required in order to force this controversial package through the Lords and which took away their right of veto, further crippling the power of the aristocracy.

There were, however, many other problems facing the Government at the time that were not so easily solved – the rising power of Germany, Home Rule for Ireland and, closer to home, the Feminist Movement. As the 20th century dawned, women became the majority of the population, they had improved health and many made the conscious decision to have smaller families and improve their lot. Around three-quarters of women between 15 and 34 years of age worked but only an exceptional few had professional jobs, most being restricted to traditional female trades like domestic service, though an increasing number were finding new opportunities in teaching, nursing, the Post Office and the new light industries. The frustration with this situation was most famously voiced by Emmeline Pankhurst and her daughters who broke away from more conservative feminist groups and campaigned with increased violence, which peaked in the years just before the First World War, a time further disrupted by widespread industrial unrest.

Middle Class Growth and Anxiety

The fear of disruption and revolution among the working classes had long been of concern to the middle classes, and now

FIG 1.5: ASHTON MEMORIAL, LANCASTER: *This huge Baroque style, domed memorial was built between 1904 and 1909 to the designs of John Belcher and was paid for by Lord Ashton, a local industrialist and millionaire.*

FIG 1.6: ST EDWARDS STREET, LEEK, STAFFORDSHIRE: *These late Victorian houses, shops and flats are cloaked in a reassuring traditional style with Cheshire black and white timber work and Tudoresque tall brick chimneys, despite this being a modern progressive industrial town at the time.*

FIG 1.7: THE FIRST GARDEN CITY HERITAGE MUSEUM, LETCHWORTH:
Some architects used features from the much idealised English country cottage, as in this example with thatched roof, rendered walls and tiny casement windows designed by Barry Parker in 1907 and now the home of the First Garden City Heritage Museum.

added to this were worries about foreign competition and moral decline, such that leading philosophers and economists predicted worse times ahead. Despite this underlying gloom the position of the professional classes was strengthened in this period with growing political influence and financial success, partly through the doubling of exports and Britain's command of the world financial markets, to the extent that the gap between the middle and upper classes closed and could sometimes merge. From the managers down to the clerks there was more money to be spent upon the home and in the rapidly increasing array of shops that had suddenly grown over the past fifty years to cater for the aristocratic aspirations of the middle classes.

The Edwardians were also surrounded by a wealth of technological advances from the past few decades, including cars, aeroplanes, the wireless and telephones. Electricity was now becoming available in more homes, its clean light and ability to power a wide range of modern appliances appealing to the middle and upper classes obsessed with hygiene and struggling to find domestic servants. In this world of machine-made products and shockingly

FIG 1.8: HAMPSTEAD GARDEN SUBURB, LONDON: *The more modest red brick country house of the late 17th century was the source for what developed into the Neo Georgian style as used in this institute and school building.*

new devices, there was a peculiarly English rejection of modernity, an obsession particularly amongst the middle classes for a mythical rural past, which had a huge effect upon interior design and architecture. This fashion for handmade crafts, rustic cottages and country ways was further enhanced by a general mistrust amongst the populace for all things Continental; even Impressionist artwork was mocked or ignored, making developments in design rather insular and backward looking.

The ideal life for the middle class family was still formalised, ordered and guided by etiquette, taught through a now wider range of books, magazines, schools and universities. Social occasions and public celebrations were embellished with pomp and deliberately elongated; all classes could take part, if only so that their position in society could be reinforced. Despite the growth and prominence of the urban middle classes they still only accounted for around 15% of the population at the turn of the century.

Working Class Life and Poverty

Life for the urban working classes, the majority of the population, had improved in many ways over the previous fifty years. The average family at the turn of the century could expect accommodation spread over four rooms rather than the one that their forebears would have had to squeeze into at the beginning of the previous monarch's reign. Life expectancy had increased with new water supplies piped to houses, improved drainage and if possible a separate privy outside for each family. Diet had become more varied, although some vegetables and fruits were not popular (jams were introduced, partly to increase the

FIG 1.9: ANITA STREET, MANCHESTER: *Working class terraced houses, maisonettes and flats now offered families more spacious accommodation and healthier living conditions than in previous generations.*

consumption as well as shelf life of fruit), and meat, which was the favourite food, was still too expensive for most families to be any more than a weekly treat.

Getting to and from the workplace was easier with the rapidly increasing tram network (there were more than 150 new systems built in this period) and the introduction of the bicycle. No longer were the lower classes confined to living within a few miles of the factory, now they too could move out to the suburbs. The factory itself was changing; a single location where all aspects of production took place was now more common, larger structures to cope with demand especially for export were built and new light industries with more tolerable working conditions appeared. There was also more leisure time – holidays to a distant seaside town or weekend jaunts into the country were within the reach of most people and the introduction of half day working on a Saturday ignited an interest in watching sport, especially football. With the formation of the Labour Party, a growth in union membership and for some the chance to vote, the lower classes now had a voice, although not an influence in the state of the country and, despite the improved situation, there was much still to voice complaints about.

Although wages had climbed, the average worker felt – with some justification – that as the cost of living had increased they had less money to spend at the end of the week, and with the volatile nature of many trades at the time their income was unreliable. Poverty was widespread, with nearly a quarter of the population struggling to make ends meet and around a tenth unable to provide for even their basic needs. Although a culture that was still guided by the Victorian self-help ethos did little

before the First World War to rectify the situation, society did at least open its eyes to the full scale of the problem. Army recruiting sergeants had noted the poor health of many of their recruits for the Boer War and benevolent individuals conducted surveys to illustrate the point, finding slum areas with high infant mortality rates even in the older established towns and cities. It wasn't just the old enemy of alcohol that was to blame, but poor diet, the quality of consumables (products like milk were often mixed with harmful chemicals to increase shelf life) and congested and unsanitary housing.

The situation was even worse in rural areas where the effects of the agricultural depression, the seasonal nature of work and Acts of God combined to restrict farm labourers' wages and keep nearly half below the poverty line. Attempts to redress the situation by providing land for growing their own produce were largely unsuccessful as few had the time or means to become small-scale farmers. Ironically the chocolate box image of tumbledown cottages draped in climbing roses with children playing outside under the watchful eye of parents, which fuelled the urban obsession with the countryside, was actually recording the squalid state of rural housing and chronic unemployment. There were, however, places that fared better; areas where farmers changed their crops to suit demand, grew fruit and vegetables or where there was dairy and sheep farming. These could all benefit from the expanding urban market, although this was dependent on good access to the rail network. Some also lived in well-constructed estate villages although they were restricted by rules and tied to their accommodation.

So the Edwardian period was one of great contrasts, when it has been

FIG 1.10: BLACK COUNTRY MUSEUM, DUDLEY, WEST MIDLANDS:
Reconstructed working class housing, complete with cobbled street and gas lighting. These houses were a vast improvement on those built fifty years before with front and rear garden and yard, and fireplaces in each room (although the upstairs ones would rarely be lit).

calculated that only 10% of the population of around 35 million owned more than 90% of the wealth and when more than 90% of the population left nothing of any great value upon their death. It was a high point in the gap between rich and poor, an era of ground breaking inventions and an obsession with the past, when modernity was wrapped up in a traditional cloak to appeal to an insecure population threatened by rapid change and foreign competition. These contrasts and past influences are nowhere more clearly on display today than the housing of the time.

CHAPTER 2

Edwardian Housing Schemes

Expansion of the Suburbs

FIG 2.1: LETCHWORTH GARDEN CITY, HERTFORDSHIRE: *This first garden city was planned with wide, tree-lined avenues radiating from a commercial core and with each house set back behind its own garden in order to bring the country into the town. This theme was continued with most houses inspired by the traditional English cottage, as in these examples, featuring dormer and casement windows, rendered walls, low-slung roofs and surrounded by hedges with picket gates. These are in marked contrast to the thousands of straight, plain, red brick terraces that were being erected in most other towns and cities at the time.*

If you started walking from the centre of most established English towns and cities you would pass through bands of progressively younger housing, from Tudor to Georgian to Victorian and finally to 20th century estates around the outside, a pattern only broken up in places by pools of older housing from

FIG 2.2: BEDFORD PARK, WEST LONDON: *A suburban private housing scheme dating from the 1870s and 80s, one of the first to be aimed at artisans and professionals. It was created by Jonathan T. Carr, a cloth merchant, who bought 24 acres of land on the edge of the city and had leading architects of the time design many of the five hundred or so houses. These were set back behind private gardens with many featuring white-painted woodwork in the fashionable Queen Anne style, which was still influential in the Edwardian period.*

settlements swallowed up in the urban expansion and from modern building inserted in prime locations or disused sites. This admittedly simplified plan seems logical but the spread of towns and cities in the past was limited by the maximum distance that could be walked to and from the workplace, invariably located in the centre, so housing for the masses could not be built on the still valuable fields miles away. Now in the wake of the Agricultural Depression many of the surrounding farms and county estates had plummeted in price and, crucially, with the expanding networks of trams, cheaper train tickets, the London Underground and even the

use of the humble bicycle this land was now viable for housing. It was in this period that the widespread expansion of the suburbs really began and it is here that most of the houses covered in this book will be found.

At the turn of the 20th century there was a boom in house building with up to 150,000 dwellings erected in a year and most of these were sited on the edges of towns. Some of the new suburban areas were developed and marketed specifically for professionals and artisans – the new middle classes, who were more aware of architectural fashions and wanted to buy into the country ideal, a home and garden bordered by fields and meadows yet

FIG 2.3: *Better quality suburban estates had wider, tree-lined streets, which either curved or were irregular in line, as in this example from Brentham Garden Suburb in Ealing, West London.*

FIG 2.4: *Most housing was still terraced or semi-detached, built in straight lines along streets laid out in grid patterns. Unlike fifty years before, nearly all houses had a front garden, even if it was only a token space like in these examples from Leek in Staffordshire, which withdrew the house back from the pavement to create a sense of privacy and grandeur.*

within easy reach of work. Tasteful, private estates with spacious and considerate planning, tree-lined roads and architect designed houses were developed within many suburbs. Some far sighted railway and underground companies whose lines had made these areas accessible worked with builders to develop the land alongside and especially around the stations, some of which were even built in empty fields before houses had even been laid out.

Most suburban estates, however, followed the pattern of the late Victorian period, generally straight rows of terraced or semi-detached brick houses along streets often laid out in grids with only retained existing roads adding irregularity. In the better quality developments, wider streets lined with trees and front gardens surrounded by a low wall with a gate were distinguishing features and, even on lesser houses, builders would try to squeeze in a small walled area to the front. For the working classes, buildings were more densely packed in to keep costs down with some of the archaic back to back houses still being erected in a couple of locations, although building regulations now stated that even these had to provide for running water, drainage and proper access for the removal of waste and ash.

FIG 2.5: *An Edwardian street may at first appear to be lined with identical houses built at the same time by the same builder, as a modern estate is. On closer inspection, though, a change in the style of windows (left-hand view) or just a staggered line of brickwork (right-hand view) illustrate that most streets were built piecemeal, in blocks, by different builders or the same one at different dates.*

The Builders

Unlike today, most of these houses were constructed by speculative builders, often just small local companies fighting with tight margins in a notoriously volatile trade. The houses they built were usually rented by tenants (only about 1 in 10 people owned their houses in the Edwardian period). The builder either acted as landlord or was paid to build them by the original landowner (who could be a college, university or the Church as well as a wealthy individual) or a developer who had purchased the site for housing. With limited capital most streets were constructed piecemeal with individual lots being developed by a number of different builders so, although a row of terraces may appear to contain identical houses, on closer inspection subtle differences in the materials and styling can indicate where one project finished and another builder or the same one continued at a later date.

Workers' Housing Schemes

In the Edwardian period it is typical to find, alongside traditional forms of terraced housing, bold, new developments which although often cloaked in a familiar Olde English façade brought new standards of space, surroundings and sanitation to the lower classes. It was philanthropists, benevolent individuals or factory owners (who appreciated the effects of good housing on their workers' productivity and loyalty) that were the driving force and finance behind these schemes. One of the earliest was Titus Salt, a Yorkshire mill owner who, during

FIG 2.6: SALTAIRE, WEST YORKSHIRE: *An early workers' village, built by Titus Salt during the 1850s and 60s to house workers from his new mill (rear left of picture). Unlike later Edwardian schemes, the houses were small terraces, tightly packed into a rigid grid pattern. However, the standard of accommodation was well above that previously available to these families and was widely admired and used as a model by other philanthropists. The village was named after Titus 'Salt' and the River 'Aire' upon which it stood.*

the 1850s and 60s, had a village built beside his new factory to house his workers. Although their homes were small and tightly packed in, around a grid layout like most Victorian housing, they did offer new standards of sanitation, communal facilities and more room than most of these families would have experienced before.

PORT SUNLIGHT

By the turn of the 20th century there were a number of other housing schemes under construction, one of the most notable being Port Sunlight on the Wirral, built by Lord Leverhulme for his workers at the Sunlight Soap Factory. The site was purchased in 1888 and during the following twenty years more than 140 acres were laid out with wide boulevards, tree-lined roads and formal gardens in a spacious and more irregular plan than the earlier Saltaire. Leading architects of the day were employed to design fashionable cottages in Queen Anne, Neo-Georgian and Domestic Revival styles, each with front and rear gardens and bathrooms, a vast

FIG 2.7: PORT SUNLIGHT, THE WIRRAL: *This workers' estate, built mainly during the 1890s and early 1900s, has moved on from the simple stone terraces at Saltaire, with architects designing attractive, spacious houses set in small groups and surrounded by gardens. These examples show the variety created, with inspiration from (left to right) vernacular cottage architecture, Tudor timber-framed houses and medieval Gothic architecture. Many of these schemes employed the leading architects of the day, the left-hand house being designed by Edwin Lutyens.*

improvement for the few that were fortunate enough to live there.

BOURNVILLE

Around the same time the Cadburys, the chocolate making Quaker family, were creating a similar estate to the south of Birmingham around their factory, which they had established in 1879. After initially building a small number of homes for his key workers, George Cadbury, appalled by housing conditions in the city, bought around 140 acres of land near the factory in 1895 and established Bournville Village. He set about building quality houses, set in groups of 2, 3 or 4, set back from the road with front and rear gardens, for what he described as honest and sober workers. Although many early examples did not feature bathrooms, they did have proper drainage, running water and an open, sunny vista, which gave suitable

FIG 2.8: BOURNVILLE, WEST MIDLANDS: *Although many of the early houses at Bournville were small terraces, later examples like this semi were more imaginative and surrounded by spacious gardens.*

applicants (who did not necessarily have to work at Cadbury's factory) a much

FIG 2.9: THE QUAKER MEETING HOUSE, BOURNVILLE: *Another feature of these housing schemes was the provision of community buildings, including shops, schools, churches and meeting places. This example was designed by Alexander Harvey, who also produced a large number of houses for the estate, and has a distinctive 'Y' shaped layout which was used on a number of large Edwardian houses and became influential in the planning of 1920s and 30s housing.*

FIG 2.10: NEW EARSWICK, YORK:
A kitchen or scullery like this one, with a small range, sink, running water and bath (with a hinged work-top above), was a luxury to the working classes of the time.

higher standard of living. In 1900 he established the Bournville Village Trust to ensure the future of his rapidly expanding community and shops, a church, a school and a village green were added to the three or four hundred houses already built at the time.

NEW EARSWICK
Another confectioner, Joseph Rowntree, a Quaker and philanthropist like Cadbury, established New Earswick, a couple of miles to the north of York, in 1902. He was responding in part to a damning report written by his son, Seebohm, into the overcrowded and unsanitary living conditions in York at the time. After purchasing the initial 150 acres he set about building mainly three bedroomed houses, with a kitchen, parlour and a living room which faced south to catch the sunlight, designed for him by the up and coming architects Raymond Unwin and Barry Parker.

Garden Cities and Suburbs
Leverhulme, Cadbury and Rowntree were in part social reformers, ahead of their time in appreciating how good housing can have a positive effect on business and society. They were not alone in their desire to improve accommodation for working families and seeing the answer in

low density, rural style estates. All three, along with many who had been involved in their projects, were to join forces in a revolutionary housing scheme that was to influence town planning world-wide – the garden city.

LETCHWORTH

The inspiration behind this project was a book published in 1898, *Tomorrow, A Peaceful Path To Real Reform*, by an English shorthand writer, Ebenezer Howard. In this he proposed ways to reverse the exodus from the country to the towns and cities by creating a new self sufficient settlement spread over 6,000 acres in which the best features of rural and urban living would combine to provide attractive and spacious housing, clean and safe factories and pleasant

FIG 2.11: LETCHWORTH GARDEN CITY, HERTFORDSHIRE: *Olde English, vernacular styled houses like these examples were more spacious, hygienic and attractive than most workers had ever experienced. Much of the housing in the city and the initial planning was the work of Sir Raymond Unwin (1863–1940) and Barry Parker (1867–1947). They began together in a local practice in Buxton, Derbyshire, before working for Joseph Rowntree at New Earswick. Their work at Letchworth and many of the other garden suburb projects around the country won Unwin the title of 'The Father of Town Planning'. He stated his aims in designing architecture as fundamentally about finding 'the form which is fit for the purpose and the circumstance of its location, with the maximum of beauty and convenience' (see also Figs 1.7 and 2.1).*

landscaped surroundings for its population, which he estimated at 32,000. His idealised town plan was compartmentalised with a central commercial and administrative centre, a separate industrial area and mixed classes of housing, with workers living around the factories and the wealthy on the edge of town. There would be shops, schools and community buildings but public houses would be permitted only if voted upon by the residents themselves (most leading reformers thought alcohol was a social evil and were supporters of the Temperance Movement, banning pubs from their own projects). It is also important to note that Howard envisaged his garden cities as private ventures, with any profit ploughed back into the community after shareholders had taken their dividend.

The interest created by the book resulted in the formation of the 'Garden City Association' in 1899, the board of which was to contain members of the Cadbury, Rowntree and Leverhulme families (Howard's book was republished in the following year under the new title of *Garden Cities for Tomorrow*). After deciding to put the ideas to practical use, the Association purchased a suitable site at Letchworth in Hertfordshire and established the First Garden City Limited in 1903. Raymond Unwin and Barry Parker, who had worked on New Earswick for Rowntree, won the competition to plan the new city and designed much of the early housing. One of the advantages with this rural site was that these forward thinking planners were free from the rigid limitations of city bye-laws, which had restricted the Cadburys at Bournville and had forced Rowntree to build New Earswick out of the town, a situation that would not be resolved until the Town Planning Act of 1909. Cottage

style houses, wide, tree-lined roads and communal buildings were erected radiating from a commercial and administrative centre along the lines of Howard's original ideas.

HAMPSTEAD GARDEN SUBURB
Garden cities as stand alone, self sufficient communities, however, were not a success, with only two being built in England (Letchworth and Welwyn), partly because companies were reluctant to up-roots and relocate from the old established centres. Instead, most of the planning and architectural features that were pioneered at Letchworth appeared in smaller suburban developments, of which around twenty were established

FIG 2.12: HAMPSTEAD GARDEN SUBURB, NORTH LONDON: *Not all houses in this scheme were inspired by the humble Olde English cottage; these grand houses designed by Edwin Lutyens around the central square were in a Neo Georgian style which was to become popular here as elsewhere after the First World War. These houses were too expensive for most and the estate mainly attracted well paid city professionals.*

FIG 2.13: HAMPSTEAD GARDEN SUBURB: *Although most garden suburb schemes had some community buildings provided, none could have surpassed those on this estate where again Edwin Lutyens designed these two huge edifices flanking either side of the central square (see also Fig 1.8). The left-hand domed building was the Free church and the right-hand the Anglican church.*

before the First World War. One of the first of these was at Hampstead, at that time on the northern edge of London. The site of around 250 acres was purchased from Eton College by the Hampstead Garden Trust, which had been founded in 1907 by a cosmetics heiress, Dame Henrietta Barnett (she and her husband, Canon Samuel Barnett, had spent much time helping the poor in the East End slums). She envisaged her village for all classes with wide, tree-lined roads, woods and gardens open to all, and houses well spaced with no more than eight per acre and surrounded by hedge-lined gardens. The Trust appointed Raymond Unwin to plan out Hampstead Garden Suburb, with Edwin Lutyens as consulting architect.

The Olde English style houses were staggered and positioned in such a way that they did not block the view of another, while the road layout contained one of the first uses of cul de sacs and now familiar names like Close, Chase and Way, which Unwin had selected because of their association with a rural, medieval world. Provision was made again for schools, communal meeting places, shops and so on, although this site is rather dominated by the two massive churches designed by Lutyens, which stand on top of the hill. Despite their best intentions the high cost of the finished houses meant that only well paid professionals from the city were able to afford to live here, a problem that blighted many such schemes intending to accommodate the working and middle classes together.

LIVERPOOL GARDEN SUBURB

Another scheme was started in 1910 at Wavertree to the east of Liverpool. As with a number of other garden suburbs it was a co-partnership scheme in which both the tenants and outside investors were shareholders, but although the rents of around 6 shillings a week were low, the initial down payment and costs of the shares meant that most residents were

FIG 2.14: LIVERPOOL GARDEN SUBURB: *A view across an open green at the centre of a quadrangle of houses on Fieldway, a cul de sac built in this garden suburb in 1913. It was designed by George Lister Sutcliffe, who had also worked at Letchworth and Hampstead, and the green area was originally intended to be a tennis court. Despite the company that developed the estate being wound up in 1938, Wavertree Garden Suburb, as it is now known, still retains its semi rural outlook and many of the features like tennis courts, bowling green and institute as was originally intended.*

reasonably well paid professionals or those who supported the project's political ideals. The early development (again done by Raymond Unwin) made strenuous efforts to retain the country lanes and mature trees on the site and build around them cottage style houses spread out at 11 per acre rather than the average of 40 in the centre of Liverpool. It was intended to be the largest such development in the country but of the 1,800 houses planned only 360 were built before the war brought construction to a halt. Most of the remaining land was sold off to speculative builders after the war and the houses purchased by owner occupiers before the company, Liverpool Garden Suburb Tenants Ltd, was wound up in 1938.

FLOWER ESTATE, WINCOBANK, SHEFFIELD

A notable development on the outskirts of Sheffield was at Wincobank where the Liberal Council upon their election in 1912 commenced building another large estate. It had curving roads, an irregular building line, houses at angles on the corners and a formal central avenue, features which had been devised at the earlier garden city and garden suburbs and which would shape housing estates in the 1920s and 30s. However, there was more at Wincobank than garden suburb. The site contains early examples of municipal housing, attempts to create cheap homes to help clear working families out of the worst areas of the city. They were just straight terraces designed in 1903–5 by Percy Houfton and H.L. Patterson, the first ones proving too expensive so the later examples were smaller with no bathroom. This was also chosen as the site for the Yorkshire and North Midland Cottage Exhibition in 1907, designed by Alexander Harvey who had worked at Bournville, and was one of a number of initiatives promoting new ideas of constructing cheap houses. The Liberal Council bought the exhibition houses but such benevolent moves were still unpopular at the time and they were booted out of office in 1908. The estate could not develop until they returned in 1912.

Municipal Housing

Cheap housing provided by local councils was limited in this period despite

FIG 2.15: ANITA STREET, MANCHESTER: *An early attempt at council-provided housing to help clear the slums. Victoria Flats in the background and Anita Street terraces in the foreground consisted of one or two bedroom flats (see also Fig 1.9) built in the late 1890s with sinks, water closets and communal laundries. Even this modest accommodation was too expensive for the very poor, so the scheme somewhat failed in its intention of housing slum dwellers. The road was originally called Sanitation Street, which reflected the importance of hygiene in society at the time. Later inhabitants didn't consider it such an attractive address and had the 's' at the front and the 'tion' at the end dropped to make it 'Anita' Street!*

incentive and legislation from the Government. The Victorian ethos of self help and the interests of local officials and speculative builders may have played some part in the disinclination by these councils to re-house working class families from the slums. There were some examples though, mainly in the large cities, where the worst areas were cleared out and new terraced housing or flats built in suburbs on cheap land. However, only respectable workers could qualify and afford to live in these first council houses. Prospective tenants were vetted for their moral and financial suitability, and had neatness and cleanliness written into their housing agreements. The rents paid were meant to be handed on in part to central government in return for financial help in the setting up of the schemes. Most of the houses and flats built were small and without bathrooms, but drainage, running water and a privy was usually a big improvement for most families.

An example of local authorities'

FIG 2.16: LANGFORD STREET, LEEK: *By the late 19th century the new houses built in Leek, as elsewhere, had to have improved sanitation. The extra cost for providing running water, drainage and more spacious accommodation increased rents while wages remained stagnant and unreliable. So despite legislation designed to improve the standard of living for working families many were still stuck in single rooms in the older slums areas (around 10% in Leek). As is often the case, it was down to local individuals and trusts to provide for the poor. In 1901 James Cornes set out to prove that through clever design and skilful construction he could build comfortable houses at low enough rents for working class families, which could still give the builder a reasonable return. He erected 50 three bedroomed houses in Langford Street and James Street (named after his sons), which attracted much interest nationally as he included a bathroom and kitchen with a patented range that served both rooms to reduce cost. Although this feature brought Cornes some success and appeared at Letchworth, the houses in Leek at rents of 5–6 shillings a week were still too high for the poorest families (accommodation was available in the town from 3 shillings a week).*

reluctance to provide housing comes from Leek in Staffordshire, where, although a new council was formed in 1894, it was made up from existing local commissioners. Their attitude towards the problem of slum areas in the town was the same as it had been before they were elected so nothing changed. It was not until the 1909 Housing and Town Planning Act, which gave local authorities the power not only to demolish slums but also to make compulsory purchases of land and erect houses, that they were forced into action.

FIG 2.17: LETCHWORTH GARDEN CITY, HERTFORDSHIRE: *A surviving house from a competition held as the garden city was just being established in 1905 to find ways of constructing cheaper houses for the masses. There were three categories ranging from £150 and including structures in brick, metal, wood and concrete. Although the prices seem low today the finished houses were if anything too well built and expensive to solve the problems of housing the poor at the time.*

This did not, however, lead directly to council houses as the Urban District Council just commissioned a report, drew up plans and then after local builders convinced them that they could provide the cheap housing sat back and watched as they didn't! In fact it made matters worse at first as the old courts and back to backs were demolished but with no new housing more families were homeless and conditions remained overcrowded!

Housing in the country was often worse than in the urban slums with, in some cases, cottages having no more than mud walls, one room, and no sink or running water. Schemes to improve the condition of rural accommodation generally failed as country landowners and farmers dominated councils and resisted change. The 1909 Planning Act allowed cottage dwellers to petition for an enquiry if their house was below standard, but after a few years only a couple of hundred houses had been built although nearly ten times as many had

been served with closing orders, which made the situation worse.

One of the persistent problems recurring throughout the Edwardian period was the attempt to design a new type of house that would be cheap enough for working class families to rent yet provide spacious accommodation and good sanitation. There were competitions and exhibitions to raise awareness and display some of the latest ideas including houses in metal, concrete and timber as well as brick. It is testimony to their designers that some of these houses still stand today, but it also highlights the problem that they built them too well and most were too expensive to attract the poorest families. One of the most positive qualities of Edwardian housing was this high standard of materials and construction, and it is these houses which still stand today with crisp edged brickwork, smooth roof lines and solid timber work that we will look at in the next chapter.

CHAPTER 3

Edwardian Houses
Materials and Structure

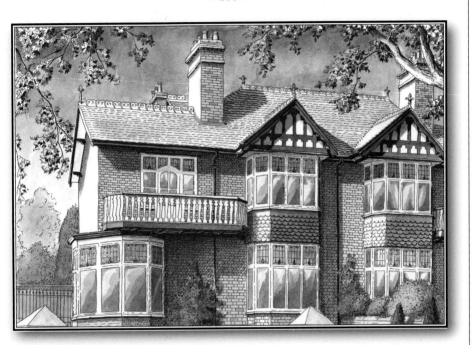

FIG 3.1: STOKE-ON-TRENT, STAFFORDSHIRE: *One half of a large semi-detached house with popular features of the late Victorian and Edwardian periods, including patterned timber gables, casement windows with stained glass uppers, and a balcony with French windows. It impresses with its size, spacious grounds, and the quality and variety of its details.*

Perhaps the most striking features of Edwardian semi or detached houses are their sheer size and quality. Large houses were tall, due to high ceilings, and wide and deep thanks to the cheap land along arterial roads and in suburban estates. Materials were generally very good although it was acceptable to save the best for the outward facing façade and use cheaper products out of sight. Even in the mass market of terraced houses – from the large three or four bedroomed town house down to the humble two up, two down – the quality of components is better than that which came before and arguably since. It therefore seems rather strange that, despite their grandeur, suburban and rural Edwardian houses, from a humble shack to an imposing detached building, were often referred to as cottages! The potent image of the countryside was seen as more of a selling point for prospective tenants or owners than their quality and size.

Materials

BRICKS

The vast majority of Edwardian houses, even in areas with suitable stone, were built in red brick with much of the production still carried out in numerous small-scale brickworks. The colour was determined by the local clay but as red was the fashion local variations in yellow, brown or white were often relegated to the sides, rear or internal walls, or those covered by some form of render or hanging tiles. The façade, however, would be in a better quality or specialised red brick and, due to the mechanisation of the brick making process and the extension of the rail network, these were now widely available and at a cheaper price. Distinctive types – like the Accrington Bloods, a hard, red brick (known as 'nori', which was iron spelt backwards) and Staffordshire Blues, a dense, grey-blue brick used for engineering works and in damp courses – could now be found across the country. New machines for extraction appeared in the late 19th century making it possible to reach the deep Oxford clays, principally around Bedford and Peterborough, which as they were naturally rich in carbon could be burnt using only a fraction of the

FIG 3.2: WAVERTREE, LIVERPOOL:
A brick terrace house with a roughcast rendered finish and flush fitted casement windows. In the past most bricks were produced locally but now with improved transport and cheaper production costs it was economic to buy them from further away. At Wavertree the bricks were bought from Letchworth in Hertfordshire rather than locally, to keep the cost of the housing down.

FIG 3.3: *It was still common to face the front of a house with the best quality bricks and then out of sight down the side to drop down to a cheaper type.*

usual amount of fuel – so these 'Flettons' were considerably cheaper. Red Builders or Tudor Reds were a high quality, sand faced brick, which could be cut with wire saws and rubbed with brick and stone into shapes for decorative pieces and elaborate chimneys.

TERRACOTTA

Terracotta was a mix of fine sand and pulverised brick or burnt clay, which was moulded into the shape or pattern before drying and firing. It could be glazed or unglazed, although the latter was the more common finish, and coloured red or sometimes cream. Most of it was produced in Staffordshire and was used for decorative plaques and tiles on the front of houses and for tiles along the ridge of the roof.

ROUGHCAST, PEBBLEDASH AND STUCCO

External rendering of brickwork had been fashionable for centuries, either to mask cheaper bricks or as a protective covering. Stucco, a general term for smooth renders, had been popular in the early and mid Victorian period as it could be grooved and painted to look like fine stonework. Now with the fashion for good quality red facing bricks it had fallen from favour but could still be found as a substitute for terracotta in decorative mouldings and plaques.

FIG 3.4: *Terracotta became popular in the 1880s and 90s and it can still be found on many Edwardian houses, not just for roof ridge tiles but also for decorative panels and plaques inserted into the brickwork.*

FIG 3.5: *A pebbledash covered wall with small pebbles and shingle set in a cement render and usually left in this unpainted finish.*

Traditional rougher finished renders were now popular on Arts and Crafts style houses, either all over the walls or just to highlight the upper storey, although it was principally for decorative effect rather than protection. Roughcast was a mixture of crushed stone or shingle with cement applied onto a surface, while pebbledash contained smaller pea shingle or stone chippings which were thrown at a cement covered wall while it was still wet. Although this has often since been painted, many examples were originally intended to be left in their natural form.

STONE

Even in areas where there was good quality building stone, brick now dominated – mainly due to cost and fashion. Local sandstone, limestone, granites and slates were still used but, due to the expense, they were often for larger, exclusive houses and public buildings or were just used for corner pieces (quoins)

or in other places in conjunction with brickwork. In areas where stone was still quarried, Arts and Crafts architects tended to incorporate them into their designs, even fragile examples like clunch (a hard chalk), as the use of local traditional materials was key to the movement's beliefs.

SLATE

With improved extraction and transport, slate – especially from North Wales – was still the most popular roofing material due to its light weight, durability (around a 100 years or so) and ease of use (it was supplied cut down to regular sizes with 20" x 10" approx being the most common). Rougher slates from areas like Cumbria were also used, though to help distribute the weight of these irregular stones the larger pieces were used on the lower section above the walls and the smaller at the top nearest the ridge.

CLAY TILES

Clay tiles were growing in popularity at this time as they harmonised with Arts and Crafts inspired houses better than slate and as they could be produced in different shapes and colours (patterned roof coverings had been very popular in the late 19th century although plain tiles

FIG 3.6: *Although houses of stone were a luxury in this period it was often used for smaller pieces in brick walls – perhaps for the quoins (left-hand view) or window and door surrounds (right-hand view). The latter picture is from Blackwell, an Arts and Crafts style house at Windermere (see Fig 4.6).*

FIG 3.7: *Clay tiles hung from wooden battens were a common decorative covering for bays on Edwardian houses.*

were now more common again). Hanging tiles vertically as a wall covering became popular from the 1880s and many Edwardian houses have a bay or upper storey highlighted by square or patterned tiles hung from wooden battens.

Structure and Construction

BASEMENTS, FOUNDATIONS AND DAMP COURSES

Basements and cellars were not common in the Edwardian period as most of the services that had been housed there in the past were now to be found in an extension at the rear or within the body of the house. In situations where they were built the site was excavated beyond the plan of the house, and walls were built up usually at a thickness of 1½ bricks lengthwise, falling back to one brick depth at ground level. The outside had a drain fitted at the foundation level and the gap was backfilled so that as much moisture as possible was run away from the basement wall.

Most houses in this period had brick foundations splayed out at the base (around 3 brick lengths wide) and then stepping back to the floor level, with many now set upon on a concrete base. Some of the rooms would have solid floors with a concrete or mortar base (typically the hall and kitchen) while living rooms usually had floorboards with air circulating beneath via airbricks (made from terracotta or iron) in the exterior walls to reduce moisture. The boards were generally thinner in width than their Victorian predecessors but were still square edged and butted up to each other.

Damp proof courses were now common and fitted between bricks a foot

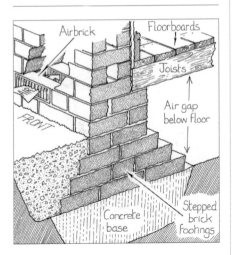

FIG 3.8: *A cut away view of the foundations of a brick house.*

FIG 3.9: *Examples of airbricks set into the lower section of the wall to ventilate under the ground floor.*

or so above ground level. There were a number of different methods although some were more successful than others. They were either a layer of tar and sand, a line of slates, sheets of lead-cored felt, or the use of impervious engineering bricks for the base of the house.

WALLS

The exterior brick walls above were nearly always one brick length thick, laid out in number of different ways. This 'bonding' can be recognised by the pattern of bricks on the outside face, made up from bricks that ran across from front to back leaving the short end exposed, the 'headers', and those that ran lengthways, the 'stretchers'. The most common bond over the past centuries and one which was still popular in this period was Flemish Bond, with alternate headers and stretchers along each course. An older form, which had been revived due to fashion and its strength, was English Bond, with alternate courses of headers and stretchers. Both of these forms could have a number of layers of stretchers between the patterned area, to use less bricks, and hence were cheaper. All of these bonds created mainly solid walls around 9 inches thick, but these tend to be susceptible to damp and are not as good for insulation as one with a cavity. Around this time Stretcher Bond, which

had been around in certain regions since the early 19th century, began to find favour, made up from an inner and outer skin of bricks with a gap between, the two sides held together by metal ties set in the mortar. This is the form that became the universal brick bond of the 20th century although the inner brick skin was replaced by blocks from the 1920s. Internal walls were either brick or stud partitions (timber framework with laths and plaster covering).

The mortar between the courses was still usually made from sharp sand and lime, and like many of the bricks of the period was slightly porous and soft. The exposed line on the outside face, the pointing, was important to the appearance of the façade and could compensate for poorer quality bricks. With sharp edged, quality bricks or 'rubbers', which could be sanded down, a fine line was achieved naturally. On less good examples a thicker mortar gap could be disguised by colouring it the same colour as the brick or adding a fine white line tucked into the wet surface (tuck pointing) to imitate better brickwork.

WINDOWS

The sash window with two glazed sashes, which could slide up and down (or sideways in the case of a Yorkshire Sash), was still popular. New large sheets of glass, which had become more widely available and cheaper in the second half of the 19th century, enabled each sash to have a single pane, but in the Revival style houses of the Edwardian period these were not appropriate, so a compromise of dividing the top half into smaller panes and leaving the bottom sash open became a distinctive feature of the time. In classical style houses both sashes were usually divided up to match the Georgian originals they were imitating.

FIG 3.10: *Examples of the common types of brick bonding. From left to right they are English Bond, Flemish Bond, and Stretcher Bond.*

FIG 3.11: *A drawing of a Victorian sash window showing the pulleys and ropes set within the frame. Note how it is recessed behind the wall in keeping with the building regulations of the time, but by the Edwardian period they could be set flush with the outer surface.*

FIG 3.12: *Three common types of Edwardian windows. From left to right they are a sash, casement and mullioned window.*

Many Revival style houses featured casement windows, ones with a hinged window (a casement) set in a fixed frame, which, although at first more expensive than a sash, were generally to replace it by the 1930s. Another form popular on Arts and Crafts houses was the long, horizontal stone window frame divided by mullions with metal casements fitted within the openings. A distinctive feature of Edwardian windows resulted from the 1894 Building Act, which relaxed the restriction of having to recess wooden frames behind the exterior wall (see Fig 3.11) so that now both sash and casement windows could be flush or even stand proud from the façade.

ROOFS

The roof was either covered in slates, which could be set at a lower pitch, or clay tiles, which due to their extra weight had to have a steeper elevation. Slates were pinned onto battens through holes and tiles hung from a nib, which were covered by the tile or slate above. There were a number of different ways the roof could be shaped. Most terraces and some semis had a straight roof with the end wall built up to support it (the gable), while some larger houses had a two stage pitch (mansard roof) which gave additional space in the attic. Hipped roofs

FIG 3.13: *Roofs were typically either a straight pitch with a gable end (left), a two stage pitch known as a mansard roof (middle), which gave extra height within the attic, and hipped (right) with the slope on all four sides.*

became popular for semis and detached houses with a slope on all four sides. Occasionally traditional thatch was used on some Arts and Crafts houses.

Plans

LARGE HOUSES

The large detached, semi or terraced houses of this period had changed in a number of ways from their Georgian and Victorian predecessors. Conditions for servants had improved as they became harder to find and retain, so basements where they had spent much of their working life were now rarities, with most service rooms in a rear or side extension and some, like the kitchen, now even built into the body of the house. The hall – which had started life as virtually the complete house in medieval times but by the Victorian period had shrunk down to no more than a narrow passage – was revived as a meeting place in many large Edwardian houses. In some, the front door opened into a sizeable, multi-purpose room while in others it was a grand central space with the main staircase leading off. Bathrooms were now standard in most houses of this class, although they were

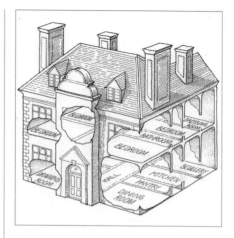

FIG 3.14: *The plan of a large late Victorian house, which like other classical styled houses of the time had a symmetrical façade with the hall in the middle.*

often still small and were usually positioned above the scullery or kitchen for ease of plumbing.

Improvements in drainage and the flexibility of a larger suburban plot helped to make the private rear garden an important feature, often included in the

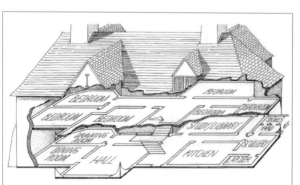

FIG 3.15: *The plan of a large, detached Arts and Crafts style house with a longitudinal layout and asymmetrical façade, with the hall as a separate multi-purpose room.*

architect's plans. This changed the appearance and plan of the rear of late Victorian and Edwardian houses compared with similar structures some fifty or a hundred years before. Rather than the rear being faced in cheap bricks and only viewed by servants, the new garden was now another part of the house so the façade overlooking it could have as much attention paid to it as the front, with any service rooms and yards hidden out of sight or masked by foliage.

MEDIUM HOUSES

The large terrace or semi, two or three storeys high and two rooms deep,

FIG 3.17: *The left-hand pair of Edwardian semi-detached houses have the doors side by side in the middle, in keeping with late Victorian practice. It was around this time, however, that builders began to site the entrances on the far ends of the façade, as in the right-hand example, for increased privacy so that after the war nearly all were built this way around.*

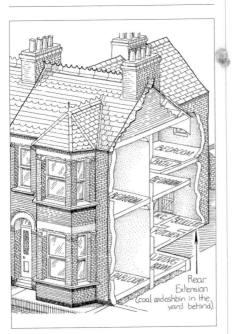

FIG 3.16: *A late Victorian medium sized terraced house with two large ground floor living rooms (the front was usually the parlour or dining room) and a rear extension with the service rooms.*

FIG 3.18: *A cut out of an Edwardian semi detached house. It is on a wider plot so there is a more spacious hall and the kitchen is fitted within the main body of the house. The example was shown for ease of illustration as it was more common for the rear extension to be on the other side so that the hall led onto the kitchen and scullery beyond.*

continued to be built for the middle classes in this period. A hall leading off the front door served two principal ground floor rooms and accessed the service rooms at the back, while the stairs led up to three or four bedrooms, an inside bathroom and separate water closet. Above this would often be an attic, which could provide accommodation for a live in servant and on the well-lit side of the house a nursery. This restricted plan, which had been so popular in the second half of the 19th century, was now dated, especially as owners found it increasingly hard to find servants and the lady of the house was reluctant to traipse up and down flights of stairs all day doing the housework.

In the better quality and more fashionable estates where a wider plot was available, larger, square planned houses were built, either detached or as a semi, typically at this date with the front doors side by side in the middle and the bays at each end of the façade. In this new layout the kitchen emerged from the cramped rear extension and became the more spacious and important room it is today, with the first range of new electric appliances putting in an appearance to make life easier for the housewife as well as the cook. As in the homes of the rich, the garden had grown in popularity and gardening in acceptability, so French windows and lean-to conservatories, which made the outside appear as an extension of the interior, were popular and any service rooms or brick stores were masked as well as possible by foliage.

SMALL HOUSES

Although many of the working classes were still living in restricted, poor quality accommodation, sometimes with the whole family in only one or two rooms,

those in well paid jobs could afford to rent one of a range of new, more spacious and sanitary houses. The vast majority of houses in this price range were two up, two down terraces erected in their thousands by speculative builders. The better examples were built in short blocks, perhaps with a token walled front space, small vestibule off the front door and good access to the rear where there could be a private garden. Cheaper houses were packed in more tightly with passageways leading to a rear yard (tunnel backs) and the front directly facing the pavement.

Inside these small Edwardian houses there would be two downstairs living rooms and two bedrooms above, one for

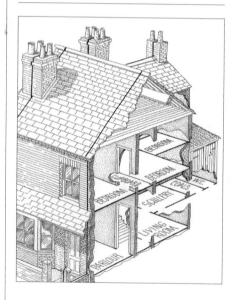

FIG 3.19: *A cut out of a small Edwardian working class two up, two down terraced house with the front door leading directly into the front living room (often used as a parlour by many families) and a central staircase.*

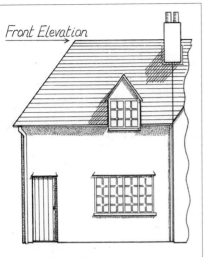

Front Elevation

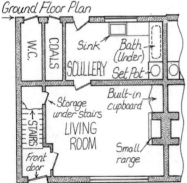

Ground Floor Plan

W.C. | COALS
Sink | Bath (Under)
SCULLERY | Set Pot
Built-in cupboard
Storage under stairs
STAIRS
LIVING ROOM | Small range
Front door

First Floor Plan

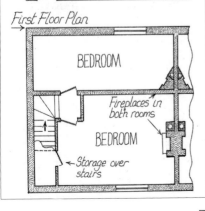

BEDROOM

Fireplaces in both rooms

BEDROOM

← Storage over stairs

the parents and the very young and the other for the older children. The better examples would have a rear extension with a scullery, coal and ash stores and a water closet, usually accessed from an outside door, while the less well off may have had to be content with a communal washroom and a brick privy in the yard.

In the Letchworth development, the garden suburbs, workers' estates and in the early council housing, there were new, more spacious designs. These could range from small semis with the scullery built into the structure, to a symmetrical block containing four or more houses, maisonettes or flats surrounded by gardens and providing two or if possible three bedrooms. Water closets were included, and some even had bathrooms, though most had a portable tin tub or a built-in bath hidden away in the scullery. Another distinctive feature of these new designs was that they were usually planned by architects so some thought had gone into the structure, proportions and detailing – which would have been of little concern to speculative builders and probably to the tenants! It is to these fashionable exterior features and details that we now turn our attention, to the notable architects and the distinctive styles that characterise this period.

FIG 3.20: *The front elevation and plans of an end terraced, two bedroomed house from a garden suburb scheme.*

CHAPTER 4

Edwardian Style
Arts and Crafts to Art Nouveau

FIG 4.1: *Arts and Crafts style semi detached house from Port Sunlight. Although the structure is that of a standard early 20th century semi the decoration is a rich display of popular, vernacular detailing like tile cladding, render, red bricks and clay tiles, although the shallow angled buttresses on the corner are rarer and a signature of this style.*

The majority of detached, semis and terraces of the Edwardian period were erected by speculative builders who had little concern for architectural correctness but more for making their buildings appeal to tenants and buyers. They were aware of the latest fashions through magazines, catalogues and the work of leading architects but although some built finely proportioned structures with up to date layouts most did not have the budget to take risks and were not concerned by the architectural quality of their work. They wanted their

Prominent chimneys sometimes sited down the slope of the roof

Gables with mock timber framing

Window frames protrude from surface.

Fine cut brick lintels

Pebbledash

Casement windows with divided top section.

Continuous roof over bay and door.

Square bays

FIG 4.2: *An elevation showing some of the fashionable features on a small to medium late Victorian and Edwardian semi or terraced house.*

FIG 4.3: *A selection of houses showing some of the features that were popular on the thousands of Edwardian houses erected by speculative builders.*

houses to sell or be rented out quickly, so they built conventional structures then applied a fashionable feature or the latest in decoration to increase their appeal. So the standard semi or terrace of the time might be branded 'Olde English', 'Tudor Cottage' or 'Quaint' depending on the theme of external decoration used. However, it was also acceptable to mix elements of the different periods up in one house, and these eclectic arrangements in the hands of less able designers are one of

the main reasons why speculative houses have received such a bad press from architects and critics alike despite their popularity with the public who choose to live in them.

For individuals who could afford it or those in charge of large housing schemes an architect would have been employed. Even in the late Victorian period these were likely to have been from a local practice but by this time it was not unusual for the best exponent of a certain style or building type to work nationwide. Their education in this specialised subject came not from schools or universities but usually by working in the office of a master architect and from simply going out and studying old buildings. Previously this would often have included a European tour but now that the country had become so insular their observations came from closer to home. This is partly why styles in this period continued to look back to a British past rather than introduce some of the more modern ideas from the Continent. Architects were also arguing between themselves about what would be an appropriate national style, resulting in the use of a variety of different periods from Britain's history for inspiration. Although some appear direct copies, many architects, by jumbling popular features of the past in new eclectic designs or by simplifying previous styles, made distinctive and sometimes surprisingly modern houses.

Arts and Crafts

This was not a style as such, but a social and artistic movement. Those who were

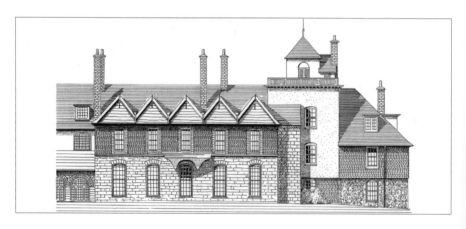

FIG 4.4: STANDEN, EAST GRINSTEAD, WEST SUSSEX (NT): *This asymmetrical arrangement of individual vernacular blocks was designed in the 1890s by Philip Webb, not the most productive of architects but one of great influence. The break from the classical symmetry really took shape with the work of Pugin and the Gothic Revival in the mid 1800s. Their belief in an honest structure meant that they were now free to plan from the inside out, creating asymmetrical compositions where the needs of the room, such as the position of a window, were put before its effect on the façade. Here at Standen he seems to have almost overworked the effect by incorporating many different finishes, including weatherboarding, brick, stone, tile hanging and pebbledash, with the intention of making it appear to have grown naturally over centuries rather than just a few years.*

grouped together under this banner produced a wide range of products, from the exotic and precious to the plain and rustic. The link, as the title suggests, was an emphasis on craftsmanship and raising its standing to that of art and at the same time improving the status and conditions of the humble worker. The movement wanted them not only to create better quality and artistic goods but also to own them rather than the tasteless, flimsy, mass-produced items on the market at the time. Arts and Crafts designers used materials in an honest way, so they were happy for construction elements to be on show and didn't use a product to imitate something else; in housing this meant real hardwood and stone rather than paint effects and stucco.

The origins of the movement began some fifty years before when the ills of industrialisation, the poor conditions of the working classes and the threat of social unrest began to inspire writers and designers to find a solution. Pugin and those who followed him rejected the foreign classical styles, with houses covered in stucco in imitation of stone, and found the beauty and honesty they sought in the Merry England of the Middle Ages. This Gothic Revival and the Victorian obsession with a mystical medieval world was further enhanced by John Ruskin, an influential writer on architecture and its effect on society, who stated amongst other key ideals of the later Arts and Crafts movement that no one should be too proud to do the simplest task: '... a painter should grind his own colours; the architect work in the mason's yard with his men'. Another who saw in ancient buildings and the traditional ways of the countryside an answer to the social problems was William Morris. He was a talented designer who founded his own company

FIG 4.5: ANNESLEY LODGE, NORTH LONDON: *This exceptional Arts and Crafts style building was designed by C.F.A. Voysey (1857–1941), a 'traditionalist' architect who looked to the past for inspiration but shaped it into new and modern forms. He was a clever self promoter who used magazines to display his work and through this inspired the next generation of architects. He spent much of his early career designing wallpaper, furniture and tiles and continued doing this work alongside his architectural commissions, which began in the early 1890s. His distinctive, simple forms with white rendered walls, shallow buttresses, low sweeping roofs and mullioned windows tight under the eaves were embellished with beautiful handcrafted details like hinges and handles, with the heart shape being a favourite motif (see Fig 5.3). His work was highly regarded in Europe and has been seen as an important element in the development of the modern movement.*

in the 1860s producing papers, tiles and fabrics for medieval style interiors, and at the same time was a socialist linking his art with political ideology and through his sheer presence and passion inspiring the next generation of artists and architects.

FIG 4.6: BLACKWELL, WINDERMERE, CUMBRIA: *This cleverly structured small country house was designed by M.H. Baillie Scott (1865–1945) on a prominent position with spectacular views over the Lake District. As with others designing under the Arts and Crafts banner it was planned from the inside out with a medieval style hall as its centrepiece complete with gallery, inglenook fireplace and beamed ceiling (see Fig 5.1). Baillie Scott was very much an individual, having little contact with other leading designers, and yet his spacious living areas and interior designs were highly influential here and on the Continent.*

The movement began to gain identity around the late 1880s in a number of artistic circles and through shows like that held at the New Gallery, London, in 1888 by the Arts and Crafts Exhibition Society after which the style was named. Guilds were formed, which attracted artists and craftsmen to live in communes offering accommodation, employment and education, the most notable being the Guild of Handicrafts, established in London by C.R. Ashbee before relocating to the Cotswold village of Sapperton in 1901. Others worked independently, like the architects C.F.A. Voysey and M.H. Baillee Scott, who not only designed the house but also every detail down to the hinges on the door and the furniture within. There are many buildings of this date that are revivals of 16th and 17th century cottages and farmhouses but those erected by these 'traditionalist' architects were different in they used these ancient sources to create new forms. Voysey's houses, for instance, are strikingly simple, proving influential to the designers of the garden suburbs and the fledgling modern movement on the

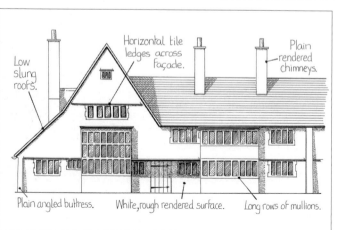

FIG 4.7: *An Arts and Crafts house of a type designed by Voysey, with labels for features that were also popular with other architects working in this style.*

Low slung roofs.

Horizontal tile ledges across façade.

Plain rendered chimneys.

Plain angled buttress.

White, rough rendered surface.

Long rows of mullions.

FIG 4.8: LITTLEHOLME, KENDAL, CUMBRIA: *This small, square, stone house, similar in form to a lodge or gatehouse, was designed in 1908 by Voysey for Arthur Simpson, an Arts and Crafts woodcarver whose work can be seen at nearby Blackwell (see Fig 4.6). Its large semicircular, arched entrance to the recessed porch (behind the gate and under the covering) was a form that proved popular on semis in the 1930s.*

Continent – and a source of inspiration to the speculative builders of 1930s semis, much to the architect's disgust!

One of the features of Arts and Crafts houses is the use of local stone and bricks in construction and traditional external wall coverings such as tile hanging, wooden shingles, pebbledash, half timbering and pargeting. Long, sweeping roofs, tall (sometimes slightly angled) chimneys covered in roughcast, horizontal mullioned windows and hardwood doors with black iron handles and hinges were also popular with a number of architects. Their interiors were perhaps more distinctive and remain influential today, with the use of lighter colours and woods, spacious open plan rooms and huge inglenook fireplaces. Although there were many variations of

FIG 4.9: *Arts and Crafts details from Blackwell (Fig 4.6) and Annesley Lodge (Fig 4.5).*

these features, most applied the general guidelines of an honest structure (where the construction and interior demands over-ruled exterior form), the use of simple forms and the enhancement of natural textures and colours.

The Arts and Crafts movement was very influential at the time and although the number of houses built using local materials and an honest structure may be few, the style they created was diluted down onto the mass housing market – many today that display their distinctive details are marketed as 'Arts and Crafts'. Despite this enduring legacy the movement was relatively short lived. Its reluctance to accept cheaper modern materials and methods of mass production made the finished work expensive and eventually ended any ideas the movement's devotees might have that art could bring about a social revolution. As Ashbee said with resignation when he was winding up the Guild of Handicrafts in 1907, 'We have made of a great social movement a narrow, tiresome little aristocracy working with great skill for the very rich.'

Olde English or Domestic Revival Styles

The design of many Edwardian houses was still influenced by the style of farmhouses and cottages from the 16th and 17th century. This trend first came to prominence in the hands of Victorian architects such as Richard Norman Shaw, who in his earlier phase created sprawling, low profile red brick houses that blended with the countryside rather than dominate it. Revivalists used the architectural details and local styles from these periods to create houses that appeared Tudor or Jacobean in origin. As with those working under the Arts and Crafts banner, exteriors were decorated

FIG 4.10: *Although houses like this one from around 1912 are often termed today as being in Arts and Crafts style, the black and white timber-framed gable and tall red brick chimneys owe more to the late Victorian revivalists in that they look as if they have been taken straight off a Tudor country house but placed in a new arrangement. This Domestic Revival style first found popularity in the hands of Sir Richard Norman Shaw (see Fig 4.12) and in the early work of Sir Edwin Lutyens (see Fig 4.11).*

with hanging tiles, mock timber framing and unpainted rendering but, rather than creating new forms inspired by the past, these revivalists tended to use exact copies of the parts and place them in new arrangements. It was the work of these architects from the 1870s/1880s – along with the Queen Anne and Arts and Crafts detailing – that was to be copied by the speculative builders in the 1890s/1900s.

Classical Styles

Edwardian architects were happier than their Victorian predecessors to use classical styles. A country nervous of increasing foreign power looked to its

FIG 4.11: HEATHCOTE, ILKLEY, WEST YORKSHIRE: *This bold and playful classical styled house owes much to Italian 16th century palaces (with perhaps a touch of Chinese in the roof design) and shows the freedom which architects could have with the classical orders compared with their strict 18th century counterparts. This masterpiece is the work of one of our greatest architects, Sir Edwin Lutyens (1869–1944). His early country houses reflected the work of Shaw and the country buildings in his native Surrey and tend to be low structures in red brick or local stone, with an ingenious use of space linking into the gardens, which were often designed by his close friend Gerturde Jekyll. It was she who introduced him to Edward Hudson, the founder of the 'Country Life' magazine, and articles featuring his houses did much to raise his profile. In the Edwardian period he began to move away from the Olde English to a blend of the vernacular and the classical in a style termed as 'Wrennaissance'. After Lloyd George's budget of 1909, country house commissions began to dry up so he became more involved in major works like Hampstead Garden Suburb (see Figs 2.12 and 2.13) and public buildings across the Empire including the Viceroy's House in New Delhi, a vast structure of classical form with local Indian style and materials. After the war he designed his most recognisable work, the Cenotaph in Whitehall (Fig 10.1) and continued with two notable projects – Castle Drogo (Fig 1.4) and the Catholic cathedral in Liverpool, which, had work not been halted by the Second World War, would have been the largest church in the Christian world (Lutyens' crypt still stands under the current 'Concrete Wigwam').*

Empire for confidence and celebrated its imperial might in grandiose buildings such as Admiralty Arch and the Old Bailey (see Figs 1.2 and 1.5 for other examples). Different types of classical architecture from the 17th and 18th centuries were used as a source of inspiration. The English Baroque style of Wren and Vanbrugh with its monumental features, richly decorated façades and domes and cupolas was popular for government, council and commercial offices. Gallic forms from the 18th and 19th centuries were also popular especially after Edward VII's close association with France.

QUEEN ANNE

This style was inspired by the smaller country house of the late 17th century (and not actually in the reign of Queen Anne) and was reinterpreted by Sir Richard Norman Shaw, the most notable Victorian architect. He made the use of red brick walls with white painted external woodwork, dormer windows, and Dutch style gables popular for urban housing, creating cheerful façades (most of the timber on the outside of a house was usually grained to look like hardwoods or painted in dark colours) that were readily copied by speculative builders in the 1890s and 1900s.

NEO GEORGIAN

Neo Georgian was based upon the simple, elegant lines of late 17th and 18th century houses. It revived symmetrical planning, plain brick façades, semicircular fan lights, and sash windows with twelve panes or more, but was also less severe, sometimes using vernacular materials and

FIG 4.12: *A late Victorian Queen Anne style house with labels highlighting some of the features that were popular with Edwardian speculative house builders. It was first developed by Sir Richard Norman Shaw (1831–1912) who had used it since the mid 1870s on projects like Bedford Park (Fig 2.2) before turning to more symmetrical, classical forms. He was a great influence on the next generation of architects, including the young Lutyens.*

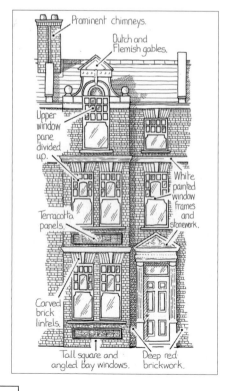

Prominent chimneys.

Dutch and Flemish gables.

Upper window pane divided up.

White painted window frames and stonework.

Terracotta panels.

Carved brick lintels.

Tall square and angled bay windows.

Deep red brickwork.

FIG 4.13: *Details from Neo Georgian houses. Hipped roofs with dormer windows and a white cornice under the eaves (left), flush fitted sash windows with twelve panes or more and doors with classical surrounds were popular on these style of houses.*

string courses, and mixing shallow arches and flat hoods on windows and dormers. Whether the house was detached, a semi or terrace the builder attempted to make the whole structure symmetrical. A notable difference from the originals was that sash windows could now be fitted virtually flush with the outside wall with the sash box around the edge exposed now that fire regulations had been relaxed; Georgian houses had them recessed behind the brickwork. With little decoration this style proved economical for even the cheapest of buildings and

FIG 4.14: *A Neo Georgian house from Hampstead Garden Suburb.*

gained widespread popularity after the First World War, especially for council housing.

Art Nouveau

This was not a distinct style but a title applied to the work of a number of independent designers across Europe. Although their art could vary from the flowing lines of Hector Guimard's Paris Metro entrances to the geometric forms in the interior designs of Charles Rennie Mackintosh, they were all linked by a desire to forge a new artistic identity not from historic sources but from nature. Art Nouveau was inspired by Japanese art with its simple forms, undulating lines and themes from the natural world (the style was named after Seigfried Bing's shop in Paris called 'La Maison de l'Art Nouveau', which sold much of this newly imported Japanese work), the Symbolists who looked to poetry and mysticism to create pictures with sensuous female figures, and to the asymmetrical, richly flowing forms of 18th century Rococo. The most characteristic features associated with this style are simple natural forms such as rosebuds or dragonfly wings, swirling stems and

FIG 4.15: *Art Nouveau style decoration from a variety of commercial and domestic buildings. Most show the flowing floral and whiplash forms that often appeared on tiles and stained glass in houses of the period, but the window on the bottom right shows the style in its geometric form as used by Macintosh (see Fig 5.10) and Austrian designers.*

branches, and figures of sinuous women with long, flowing hair. Artists were not afraid to produce work for the aristocracy or to adapt their designs for mass production. In architecture it was their prominent use of modern materials like glass, steel and concrete that set them apart from their contemporary Arts and Crafts idealists back in England.

Although its origins lay on these shores in the writings of John Ruskin, the work of William Morris and the furniture designs of Arthur Heygate Mackmurdo,

Art Nouveau made little impact here, partly due to our dislike of foreign styles and obsession with the past. Furniture, silverware and light fittings featuring sinuous forms from nature could be found in the more cosmopolitan middle or upper class household, but the exterior of houses was rarely inspired by this style. What can be found are its flowing natural forms within stained glass windows, glazed tiles in porches, pargeting within gables, terracotta panels and door furniture.

FEATURES FROM THIS PERIOD

FIG 4.16: *A distinctive feature of Edwardian houses was the positioning of the chimneys directly above the fireplaces in the front and rear rooms so the stacks appear halfway down the slope of the roof.*

FIG 4.17: *A selection of late Victorian and Edwardian balconies and verandas. They were typically made from turned or carved balusters painted white, some with French windows making them accessible (no 5) but others being purely decorative (no 3).*

FIG 4.18: *A selection of late Victorian and Edwardian porches and details. Simple recessed doorways with ceramic tiles up the inner sides (nos 2, 3 and 6) and external white painted wooden structures some with elaborate patterns which were available in kit form to builders (4, 5, 8, 9, 10, 11, 12, 14 and 15) were both popular. Continuous porches between gables were also common (1 and 7) while some Arts and Crafts houses had deeply recessed doorways with large arched openings (13).*

FIG 4.19: *A selection showing the wide range of styles of late Victorian and Edwardian doors. They were typically side by side in terraces and semis at this date (2, 3, 4, 6, 11 and 16) and usually still had a larger top half, which could be either single glazed (1, 5 and 8) or broken up into smaller panes (6, 7 and 16). Arts and Crafts houses often had simple, plank doors (13, 14, 17 and 18), the finest with decorative door furniture and elongated strap hinges (14). A small single window to the side of the door (7, 11, 15 and 18) was usually fitted on suburban houses, which could now have a wider, spacious hall due to the cheaper land. Hardwood doors were best but most were made in cheaper woods and either stained to look like a superior wood or painted in a dark colour (green, brown and black were popular), sometimes with the edges or panels picked out in a white or cream (6). Door furniture was either in brass or black iron, the latter popular as it required less cleaning. Letter plates were small due to the size and limited quantity of post and were either brass or iron and often with a decorated border and with 'letters' stamped in the middle.*

FIG 4.20: *A selection showing the wide range of styles of window that could be found on late Victorian and Edwardian houses. Large panes of glass were now cheap and widely available, giving a clear view for all, but these did not suit the retro style of houses so a compromise of an open lower and a divided or patterned upper was common. These could either be sash windows (1 and 9) or casements (3 and 8), with stylised floral stained glass a popular choice in the latter (4, 6, 7 and 15). Windows since the 1890s could be flush fitted or stand proud (6, 8, 11, 16) while double storey bay or bow windows were used on large and medium sized houses (1, 9, 10 and 14) with simple, single storey ones on some smaller dwellings. The wide choice of window design can be seen in the materials used (7 and 13) and in different shapes and forms (12 and 15) like the eyebrow dormer (2), which became popular after the war. Exterior blinds were often fitted, although only the box at the top of the window often remains (11) and shutters were also popular (16), both helping to protect interior decoration and furniture from sunlight. White painted windows had become popular with the Queen Anne style although many were still either stained to look like hardwoods or painted a dark colour with the inner edge highlighted in white.*

FIG 4.21: *A selection of stained glass door panels and windows showing the popularity of stylised floral patterns. Sometimes stained glass was used just for a simple border around the edge of a window (2), at other times it could be used to make complex and elaborate pictures in the finest houses (11).*

BLAKEMERE

FIG 4.22: *A selection of gable ends showing the wide range of styles and materials used. Timber-framed patterns (1–3) were probably the most common, but designs with hanging tiles (6), rough cut timber (7), brick and terracotta (9) and pargeting (8), a raised plaster design, can also be found. Bargeboards, which are fixed vertically to protect the exposed end of the roof, tend to be simple in design compared with the elaborate mid Victorian types, with either a straight edge (1 and 3), a shaped edge (4 and 5) or simple perforations (2). The Dutch style gable (10) was usually found on Queen Anne style houses from the 1880s and 90s but was still built in the Edwardian period.*

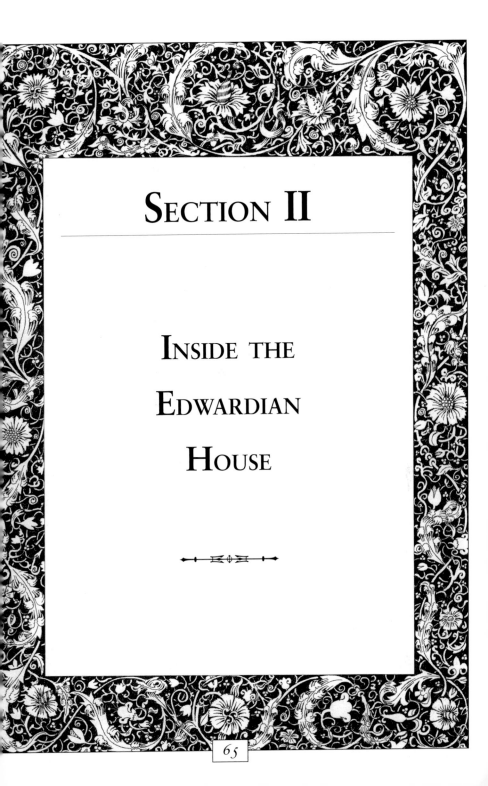

SECTION II

INSIDE THE EDWARDIAN HOUSE

CHAPTER 5

Interior Fittings and Decoration

FIG 5.1: BLACKWELL ARTS AND CRAFTS HOUSE, WINDERMERE: *The hall which greeted visitors to this family country retreat designed by Baillee Scott was inspired by medieval types with its double height and a gallery above the large inglenook fireplace (rear left) and the architect's popular black and white timber work. The control of space and light is remarkable, making the room both imposing and yet intimate. The two tone banding in the arch above the fireplace comes from the use of sandstone and slate, both supplied locally in keeping with Arts and Crafts practice.*

Fashionable Edwardian interiors reflected the trends for light, cleanliness and simplicity. Sunshine was brought into the house with carefully positioned windows and paler coloured walls. Hygienic materials that wouldn't show dirt were the order of the day now that servants were so hard to find. Decorative designs were less complicated and furniture and ornaments neatly

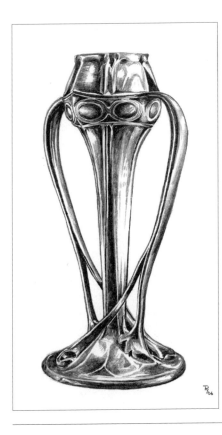

FIG 5.2: *A piece of silverwork blending Celtic and Art Nouveau forms and supplied by Liberty's in the early 1900s. This influential shop was founded by Arthur Lazenby Liberty who was born in 1843 to a draper from Chesham in Buckinghamshire. After divorcing his first wife he became engaged to Emma Louise Blackmore whose father helped him fund a new shop at 218a Regent Street, which opened in1875, specialising in oriental art, silver artefacts, fabrics, and furniture. As he grew successful he also had exclusive pieces designed for the shop with the creators remaining anonymous as all products were over-stamped with 'Liberty and Co' and many were machine made, even those sold under the Arts and Crafts banner. He was so successful that he bought a 3,000 acre country estate in Buckinghamshire and even had a marble seat installed at Marylebone station for his use while he waited for the evening train!*

grouped rather than giving the appearance of being scattered as in Victorian houses. In the hands of Arts and Crafts architects, who involved themselves in the interior design even down to details like door hinges, the rooms could be painted white with light woods, stone and brick shown off in their raw colours, a stark contrast to the typical house of the time.

Those households who were concerned with the latest in fashion found it increasingly easy to gain access to the latest styles of fabrics, wallpapers and fittings through new magazines, the Ideal Home Exhibition, which started in 1908, and most importantly through shops like Liberty's and Heals. Some of these shops imported popular fabrics, rugs and decoration from Japan, India and the Continent and at the same time were an outlet for products from the leading English designers, including mass produced lines. They were happy to have items made for them under the Arts and Crafts banner but did not buy into the craftsman ethic. Middle class homeowners could now buy previously exclusive products and display their refined taste back in their suburban semi or terrace. Even the better off working class family could aspire to interiors that were more than just functional. There was now scope for Edwardian interiors to show greater daring than the rather conservative and traditional exteriors.

STYLE

Art Nouveau, which rarely shows its face outside, was a popular source with elongated foliage patterns appearing on tiles, glass, fireplace surrounds, stencils and on fittings such as lamps. Materials that were previously seen as utilitarian – copper, pewter and iron, for example –

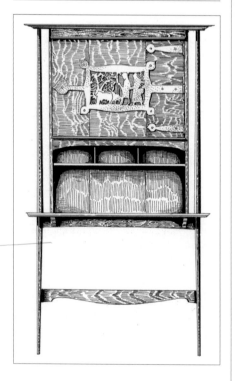

FIG 5.3: *An elegant Arts and Crafts style oak cabinet by Voysey with decorative strap hinges featuring the architect's favourite heart motif and a large medieval rural scene in the centre.*

could now be used for decorative items in reception rooms. Arts and Crafts designers influenced homeowners although only the rich could afford the expensive woods and handmade goods they used. Magazines, exhibitions and shops displayed their interiors, which included simple forms, lighter colours, materials shown in their natural tone and texture, and care for even the smallest of details. They tried to banish freestanding furniture from their interior designs and created fixed pieces and built-in cupboards especially around the fireplaces that were the centrepiece of their schemes. Japanese tastes still influenced the Edwardian home, especially with the popularity of ebonised (black lacquer or stain finish) furniture and woodwork. Interiors of the 18th century, with decorative mouldings, pale coloured walls and grand fireplaces, became fashionable again in similarly styled houses. Reproduction Georgian and Regency furniture was generally popular and, although trend-setting manufacturers looked to more modern, lighter and simpler designs, it was styles from the past that reassured the mass public.

However, the speculative builders and many homeowners of conservative outlook would probably keep to a fairly safe and traditional format for the interior. There were practical considerations such as the dirt from coal dust in the air, mud brought in from unmade roads (although most estates had pavements now to reduce the problem) and soot from gas and oil lights, which led to dark coloured surfaces and busy decorative elements still being used for concealment purposes. Few could afford the materials used by top designers so even in Arts and Crafts inspired interiors cheaper woods were stained to look like

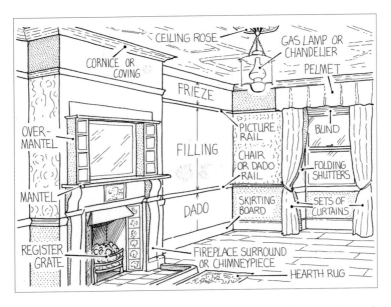

FIG 5.4: *A drawing of a living room with labels highlighting the parts featured in this chapter.*

more luxurious hardwoods, and materials like metals, pine and cheap stone were painted to imitate marbles. In all houses there was a distinct order of decoration – with the impressing of guests as the top priority. In today's more socially open houses the most money is often lavished upon the kitchen; in the Edwardian house, however, visitors would never see the service rooms and would rarely go upstairs so it was in the entrance hall, dining and drawing rooms where the more elaborate mouldings and expensive fittings were to be found. If you are trying to discover the former use of rooms, it is useful to look at the original cornice, skirting, doors and fireplaces (eg Figs 6.6 to 6.9).

FIREPLACES

The most important feature in a room was the fireplace. It was not only the main source of heat but also the focal point of the room. It consisted of a grate in which the coals or wood were held and the surround or chimneypiece, which could range from a luxurious marble creation to a single piece cast iron. As with all decoration the best were saved for the main reception rooms, and cheaper versions for upstairs, while lesser bedrooms and attics may have had none at all, with just a thin chimneybreast from a downstairs room passing through on the way up. It was common in Edwardian houses for there to be individual chimneystacks running straight up and out halfway down the slope of the roof rather than meet in the middle before emerging on the ridge (see Fig 4.16). The pots, which originally would have been fitted with a variety of cowls and deflectors to improve the draw, can give some idea of how many fireplaces there would once have been and where they were sited, if they have since been removed.

GRATES

This is the term for the cast iron basket, back and sides that held the coals. The most popular type, which could be found in most houses, was the register grate. These had a hinged plate (the register) set above the fire – the draw was adjusted by opening or closing the access to the chimney – and had been around since the late 18th century, but it was not until the late Victorian period that they became reasonably efficient with a series of new features. The cast iron grate now had splayed sides, which were usually tiled, to help reflect the heat into the room. An adjustable vent was fitted in the ashpan below to help the fire burn evenly and produce less pollution, a great concern at the time as consumption had multiplied many times and the great fog of 1880, which killed 700 people, was caused by coal fires. The basket had also been pushed further out into the room so less heat was lost up the chimney and a built-in or separate hood, often in beaten copper, was fitted above the basket to keep the smoke out.

Despite its efficiency, older types were still to be found, especially freestanding dog grates in which was burnt wood, much advocated by Arts and Crafts architects. They preferred the old fashioned log fire to coal, which was seen as part and parcel of the machine age, and these types of grate fitted in better with the large open inglenook fireplaces, which were a distinctive feature of their medieval inspired halls (see Fig 5.1).

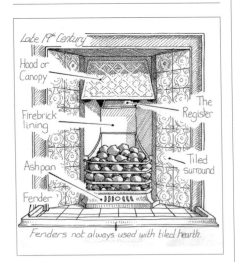

FIG 5.5: *A register grate with labels of the parts.*

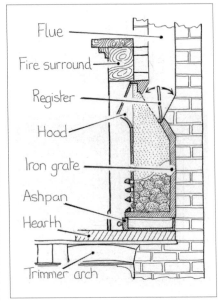

FIG 5.6: *A section through a register grate showing its interior arrangement.*

FIRE SURROUND

The decorative fire surround was available in a wide choice of styles to reflect that of the building or room. Art Nouveau inspired elongated foliage designs could be found running up the sides of cast iron surrounds, or Arts and Crafts tiles on the splayed cheeks of the grate with floral, animal, medieval or exotic patterns and even blue and white Delft designs.

For the best rooms, marble (red and grey or black) and hardwood (oak and mahogany) types were preferable, but if these were too expensive then slate painted to imitate marble and pine stained to look like a better wood were used. Cast iron surrounds were widely available, either as one piece including the grate for less important rooms or as a substitute for better quality materials where they could be black leaded, burnished silver or painted in a white marble effect. Arts and Crafts houses could feature surprisingly exotic fire surrounds from classical, Islamic or Japanese sources, in addition to types in a lighter wood or painted white or cream. They also had large inglenook fireplaces in either stone or brick with seating and cupboards fitted to the sides. In others the vertical brick chimneybreast was the feature, with just a small recess at the bottom containing the fire.

The mantelpiece still tended to be deep, a late Victorian fashion, which allowed an ever-growing array of ornaments and photographs to be displayed. Another feature that was still in fashion was the overmantel, a continuation of the

FIG 5.7: *A detail from an Edwardian cast iron fire surround with foliage patterns in the casting and Art Nouveau style tiles on the splayed sides.*

FIG 5.8: *Examples of fireplaces ranging from the simple and modern type in no 1 to the elaborate Arts and Crafts style arrangement with built in seating, side window and small glazed cupboards in no 2. No 4 is a small cast iron piece with Art Nouveau detailing and no 5 is a mock marble effect with brass accessories. Nos 3 and 6 are polished metal smoke hoods.*

FIG 5.9: *Examples of wooden Edwardian fireplaces. Additional shelving for ornaments either above or below the mantelpiece and mirrors built into the overmantel were common features. A chimney cloth (bottom right) was often hung from the mantelpiece – originally it was to keep smoke out of the room but by this date was purely decorative.*

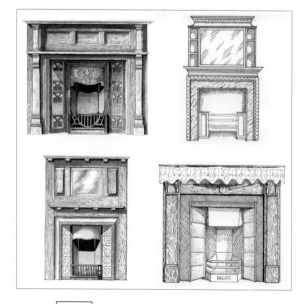

FIG 5.10: *A remarkably modern style of fireplace by Charles Rennie Mackintosh. He, along with designers at Darmstadt in Germany and Wiener Werkstatte in Vienna, found inspiration from geometry in nature, favouring simple, elegant shapes and patterns with straight lines and gentle curves. It was these forms that, as Art Nouveau faded, became the inspiration for the Art Deco and Modernism of the 1920s and 30s. Unfortunately Mackintosh's reputation for unreliability, eccentricity and drunkenness put off customers in his own lifetime and he was not appreciated on these shores. The success he did find in Austria created further problems with the outbreak of war and it is only in more recent years that his work has become iconic.*

surround above the mantelshelf, usually with a large central mirror (these were popular now that plate glass was much cheaper) and some type of shelving to the sides. It was still common to find a chimney cloth or smoke deflector, usually a light coloured embroidered fabric, which was draped down over the mantel and although it was originally used to keep the fumes out of the room it was purely decorative at this date.

GAS FIRES

In the days before central heating the fire had to be reliable and efficient, and this was not true of the early types of gas fire, which appeared on the market around this time. They had a reputation for blowing out, being expensive to run and having a supply that was still not available everywhere, and hence they tended not to be popular.

STAIRS

In larger Edwardian houses the stairs were made a feature, whether they were positioned centrally, as they often were in symmetrically fronted Neo Georgian

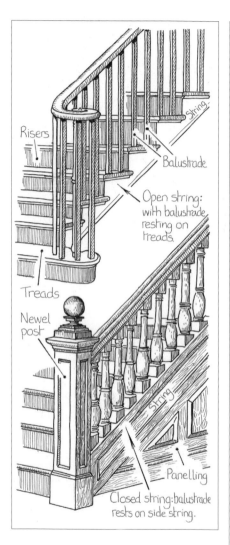

Risers

Balustrade

Open string: with balustrade resting on treads.

Treads

Newel post

String

Panelling

Closed string: balustrade rests on side string.

FIG 5.11: *Drawings of a Regency style open string and a late Victorian closed string staircase.*

post and balustrades elaborately carved, although once the first floor was reached the detailing was often simplified as it was out of sight of guests. Again there were a variety of period styles of balustrades and handrails that could be chosen, from the popular heavily carved Jacobean to the simple, fretwork types used by some of the Arts and Crafts architects. Most were wood, sometimes mixed with a polished hardwood for the handrail and cheaper painted or stained pine for the balusters, and there were also some in cast iron.

Some stairs were still open string, whereby the balusters sit upon the horizontal treads, but most were of the closed type with the tread set into the diagonal side panel upon which the balusters were fixed. It was also common for the underside of the latter type to be boxed in, often with wood panelling to match the hall. Anaglypta or lincrusta relief (textured) papers – these were trade names that have passed into general usage – were popular for the lower section of the wall up the stairs with either a handrail or dado rail. A large vertical window often illuminated the staircase but to ensure privacy from neighbours the glass was usually stained or frosted with some elaborate patterns and designs, making this an outstanding feature on many late Victorian and Edwardian houses.

In the more modest home, where space was limited, the stairs could be squeezed into a corner or trapped between two walls in the centre of the house, leaving little opportunity for decorative balustrades. The mass production of turned wood parts meant, however, that where a hall was wide enough an ornate staircase was affordable. There were also decorative possibilities around the bottom of the stairs where fretwork

style houses, or to the side or rear of the hall in many other types. The bottom steps could be enlarged and the newel

FIG 5.12: *Examples of staircases from the simple Arts and Crafts style (left) to a more elaborate Jacobean type with panelling below (right). The centre picture shows a tall stained glass window, which illuminated the stairs and was a feature of most larger houses.*

arches or turned wood screens were fashionable.

INTERIOR DOORS

The standard Victorian four panelled door (two large upper panels and two small lower ones) was still common in Edwardian homes. The better quality examples for more important rooms had fielded panels consisting of a raised piece in the centre with moulding round the edge, and flat panelled versions, with or without moulding, were used in less prominent situations. Again the best doors were hardwood with cheaper pine ones stained to look like it, while in more fashionable interiors they could be ebonised or painted (some with different colours to match the room and mouldings picked out in cream or gold). Arts and Crafts designers tended to use lighter woods such as ash and yew, polished but not stained. Some, including the front

door, had upper panels filled with glass, which could be stained for those facing outside and frosted or etched when between rooms, while solid doors could have stencilling and paper patterns as decoration. Other designs available included a return to the six panelled door in classical interiors and plank and batten doors in some Arts and Crafts houses, with the only decoration coming in the form of elongated strap hinges or crafted iron handles. This latter type was also used on most working class houses although at the front on better examples there might be a simple form of panelled door.

Door knobs and handles were available in wood, brass, ebony, white china or glass on the most important doors with the cheaper materials and less decorative forms elsewhere. Black door furniture became popular too as it required less cleaning. Fingerplates to protect the door

FIG 5.13: *A selection of interior doors from the elegant hardwood types (left and right) to the plain plank and batten door used between service rooms (centre).*

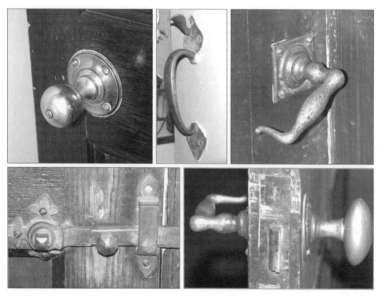

FIG 5.14: *Iron and brass door furniture. Note in the bottom right picture how the more ornate door handle to the left faced out into the hall where a guest would have entered but there was just a plain knob on the other side.*

where it was pushed open were still fitted and available with highly decorative patterns and edging. Now that mortice locks set into the door were common, escutcheons to cover the keyhole were fitted, usually in a tear-drop or oval shape and again matching the material used for the knob. Arts and Crafts houses with more humble plain doors were usually fitted with black iron handles and strap hinges, with a beaten finish and decorated with a motif or pierced shapes.

CEILINGS

As with most decoration in the Edwardian house, the patterns and designs became simpler compared with their Victorian predecessors. This is true of the ceiling, partly as shallow and less complicated mouldings did not require as much cleaning and also to suit the current fashions. Ceilings were still made of plaster pushed through onto laths (thin strips of wood), which were pinned to the underside of joists, with the finished surface either left plain, fitted with shallow mouldings in the corners or covered with a patterned relief paper like anaglypta (ceiling roses had generally fallen from use by this date).

FLOORS

Floors were either wooden planks or solid, usually concrete with some form of tiled covering. Floorboards were narrower than 18th and early 19th century types and were laid at right angles to the joists with an air gap below to help reduce damp. The quality of the house or room can be reflected in the way the boards were nailed down; in the best the nail heads were hidden by being hit at an angle into the cut end, but the more usual method left them visible on the top surface (mass produced tongue and groove boards were also becoming

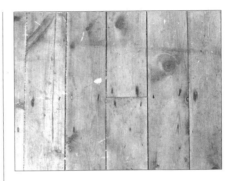

FIG 5.15: *Floorboards in Edwardian houses tend to be narrower than those a century before. In most the nail heads are exposed on the top face as here, but in the finest houses they could be hit through at an angle in the cut end and hidden from view.*

available now). Most floorboards were of pine and deal, stained or painted a dark colour in important rooms or scrubbed white if in service areas or bathrooms.

Solid floors were common in the hall and some ground floor rooms and could have a number of different coverings including mosaics, terrazzo, stone or wooden parquet, although tiles were the most popular. These could be plain red or black quarry tiles (from the French word 'carré' meaning square), geometrics, which came in different coloured squares and triangles to form designs, or encaustics, which were decorated tiles with different coloured slips poured into a stamped pattern before firing fused it together. In spite of the fact that a wider range of colours was available, black and white geometric patterns along the hall or on the porch were very popular. Although durable the unglazed surface had to be polished and sealed after cleaning, usually with linseed oil and a coat of wax.

FIG 5.16: *Examples of floor tiles, from the elaborate patterns of geometric tiles found in the hall to the plain black and red quarry tiles usually laid in the service areas.*

Another popular covering was parquet flooring, sheets of thin blocks of wood or veneers arranged in patterns and ready to lay. They provided a quality finish and what was perceived as a hygienic, easy to clean surface. Linoleum, a compressed mixture of cork, sawdust, oils and glue on a canvas backing with a surface imitating better quality floors, was popular in bedrooms, bathrooms and nurseries.

It was common for most surfaces to have a scattering of rugs, which were still preferred to fitted carpets – both because of fashions set by Arts and Crafts designers and because they could be easily lifted and cleaned outside (important in the days before vacuum cleaners). Oriental rugs and handwoven carpets could be found in the finest homes though floorcloths and rag rugs were more common. Floorcloths were made from a

FIG 5.17: *Parquet flooring.*

canvas backing treated with various substances to imitate a woven rug or carpet and were now widely available and cheaper. Rag rugs were made from pieces of old cloth, cut into strips a few inches long and then pushed with a sharpened peg into the holes in a sheet of sacking or hessian. They were used in less important rooms and in front of the fire, and were common in working class houses. Loose carpets were reserved for the best rooms and the first flight of stairs; however, fitted versions, which had fallen from favour, made a comeback in the houses of the rich where there were servants on their hands and knees with brushes and dustpans to clean them.

WALLS

Internal walls were plastered in layers, either directly onto the stone or brickwork or onto horizontal laths in the case of some dividing walls, with the finished surface edged and divided up by various mouldings. From top to bottom

these were: the cornice or coving, which covered the gap between wall and ceiling; the picture rail, which could be quite low at this date, running in line with the top of the doors; the dado or chair rail designed to protect the wall from furniture but purely decorative in Edwardian houses; and the skirting around the junction of wall and floor. All or just some of these could be used, depending upon the architect or builder, although the picture rail is more common than the dado in principal rooms. Arts and Crafts designers tended not to use wall mouldings, preferring wooden panelling. This traditional wainscot was comprised of vertical boards, usually of oak, built into frames, running around two-thirds of the way up the wall with a plate rail capping it off. In revived classical style houses rectangular moulded frames were fixed to the wall to create a light panelling, which was then painted to match or co-ordinate with the colour of the wall or picked out in white.

FIG 5.18: *Examples of cornice, picture rail and door surround. These were generally shallower and less ornate than mid Victorian types.*

FIG 5.19: *Examples of floral patterned wallpapers that could be found in late Victorian and Edwardian houses. Some were the work of leading designers including William Morris and C.F.A. Voysey, or those working anonymously for companies like The Silver Studio or shops like Liberty's.*

WALLPAPER

The most popular wall covering in Edwardian houses was still wallpaper. After the Victorians had perfected mass production techniques it had become cheaper and widely available, although the patterns were now more simple and stylised and set upon lighter colours than before. Designs containing themes from nature were the most common, with patterns of mainly flowers and foliage but also fruits and birds, the paper often matching curtains and furnishing fabrics. Quieter patterns, which acted as a background to pictures rather than dominating them, began to come into fashion. Paper was usually run up to the picture rail with the frieze above either painted and stencilled or covered in a wallpaper design specifically for this position.

Relief papers like lincrusta and anaglypta were popular for the dado especially in areas of hard wear like the hall. Lincrusta was produced by the same company who made linoleum but used wood pulp rather than cork, while anaglypta was an embossed paper, which made it lighter and more versatile. The finished surface was painted and sometimes varnished for extra protection.

FIG 5.20: *Examples of late Victorian and Edwardian relief papers, which were popular on the frieze above the picture rail, the dado in the hall and up the stairs and on some ceilings.*

Painted walls were usually found in less prominent rooms like the kitchen, scullery, bathroom and smaller bedrooms, although in Arts and Crafts and Neo Georgian houses principal rooms were often painted, setting the 20th century fashion for plain walls. Most people employed a decorator to do the painting, many of whom still made their own colours, although ready mixed tins of paint were now available. Colours tended to be less intense than the vivid shades of the mid Victorian period; plum, pinks and greens were popular in conjunction with white and cream, pale blues, greens and greys in Neo Georgian and plain off-white walls in Arts and Crafts houses. Stencilling was often used, especially along the frieze.

WALL TILES

Ceramic wall tiles were widely available – either glazed, with a transfer printed pattern, or with an embossed design.

Decorative tiles were used up the splayed sides of the fireplace or in the hall or porch in conjunction with plain ones. Plain whites, which would show up any dirt, making it easier to clean, were used in the kitchen and bathroom. Handmade tiles were reintroduced by Arts and Crafts architects, who included the design of them in their portfolios.

WINDOWS AND CURTAINS

Curtains and blinds were not only important for privacy and to keep out draughts, but also to protect furniture and furnishings from sunlight. In the front windows of most upper and middle class homes there would have been three layers, from an outer blind to a fabric inside, while more modest houses could have nets on the lower half of a sash window with simple curtains behind. In windows that were away from the glare of the sun and out of public view a single blind or curtain or both would have

FIG 5.21: *Examples of glazed tiles, from Arts and Crafts handmade tiles with colourful displays of foliage and birds to plain brick shaped tiles, which in this case were used in areas of hard wear like the porch, the hall, or in the service rooms.*

sufficed. Curtains were either plain or patterned; floral designs were popular, especially chintzes (glazed printed fabrics) which often matched the wallpaper in the room, and also silks, damasks and muslin. Many had pelmets above covering the rail, which could be boxed types fitting in with the frieze or covered in the curtain fabric and finished with trimmings like tassels. Arts and Crafts designers were influential in promoting these lighter weight fabrics, which they usually hung on simple brass or wooden poles.

LIGHTING

Illuminating rooms in Edwardian houses was often done with a number of dif-

ferent lighting types rather than one. Gas was the main source of light and it had grown in popularity since the improved mantle designs of the 1880s made them brighter, or more importantly they could produce the same light as the old types but with the supply turned down so they were cheaper and less dirty. Now even the working classes might have one or two gaslights as penny slot meters were introduced. The lights could be fixed to the wall with the mantle facing down and a shade above (earlier types had the mantle pointing up), or hanging from the ceiling as a single light or decorative chandelier. Freestanding table gaslights and standard lamps were also available connected by flexible rubber tubes.

FIG 5.22: *Examples of gaslights and the wall brackets, which can sometimes still be found.*

Oil lamps were another popular source of light, although they produced only a third of the brightness of gaslights. They were usually filled with paraffin (distilled from coal) and being portable were more flexible than gas, both as table lamps or hanging from the ceiling. Candles were still used in more modest and rural houses, from cheap tallow ones dipped in animal fat to the better quality paraffin and beeswax.

Electric light had previously been found only in the wealthiest houses due to limited supply and expense. Early bulbs were weak by modern standards and it was not until new incandescent types were introduced in 1907 that it really began to find favour. It was clean, bright and cheap to run and became an aspiration for the middle classes. Although the light produced was only equivalent to a 25 watt bulb Edwardians often covered them with richly decorated brass, copper or coloured glass shades to cut out the glare!

FIG 5.23: *A glass and metal lamp from Tiffany – their distinctive Art Nouveau style lighting with colourful displays of glass was very popular at the time in fashionable interiors and is still widely copied today.*

CHAPTER 6

Living Rooms

FIG 6.1: BROAD LEYS, WINDERMERE, CUMBRIA: *One of the principal rooms, currently used as a lounge, in the largest of C.F.A. Voysey's houses overlooking Windermere. One of its distinctive large bow windows can be seen in the rear through the archway. It is now the headquarters of the Windermere Motor Boat Club.*

Large and Medium Houses

HALL

The first space that visitors to an Edwardian house would have entered was the hall, and one of its main purposes was to impress upon them the wealth and standing of the owner.

Halls could range from a large open space in the grandest house down to a narrow passage in the more modest. Wider plots in the suburbs enabled the latter class of house the possibility of fitting in a small front window, a more elaborate and prominent staircase, seating, occasional furniture and even a little fireplace. The better sort of working class house too began to incorporate a square space that helped keep the draughts out of the living rooms as well as raise the tenants' status. A notable change in this period was the reintroduction by Arts and Crafts architects of the hall as a central living room, a retro medieval hall with a large, often recessed fireplace (inglenook) with seating and even a dining table and chairs in some of the largest (see Fig 5.1). In the suburban semi or terrace, half halls, which ran to the middle of the house with the service rooms beyond, were a popular arrangement.

In most houses the hall would still have been a passageway – of varying width but with many fashionable similarities in decoration. One of the most distinctive features of late Victorian and Edwardian halls was the solid decorative floors, which could have been marble, mosaic, terrazzo or encaustic tiles in the finest houses, or patterns made up with geometrics (triangles and diamond shapes) and plain squares in many others. These were cheaper and more widely available, and there was a greater choice of colours although black and white became popular at the same time. In some, a runner (a long, thin rug) was placed down the hall especially where the floor was boarded, in which case they were usually stained a dark brown to imitate a hardwood.

Due to the wear and tear of people passing through and the dirt and soot brought in from outside, the narrow hall was usually decorated in strong colours and with durable materials. The dado could have been tiled or covered with lincrusta, anaglypta or a similar tough paper, which was then painted in a strong colour, sometimes a shade of the one that was used in the main room which led off it. A dado and picture rail were usually fitted (or just one or the other) and the

FIG 6.2: *Late Victorian and Edwardian halls often featured dramatic geometric tiled floors, as in this example from a medium sized terrace house.*

wall between decorated with a neutral coloured paint or patterned paper so as not to clash with the decor in the house. These materials could all be varnished afterwards for protection and to make them easier to clean. The frieze above the picture rail and the ceiling were usually painted in white, off-white or cream.

On longer halls there would have been an arch with simply styled brackets, which usually carried the central load-

FIG 6.3: *A wider hallway with black and white tiled floor, relief paper covering the dado, and a simple patterned paper above this. The stairs have more room than in Victorian houses of this class and a decorative newel post and balustrade can now be fitted, with the door leading to the service rooms at the rear.*

FIG 6.4: *A relief paper covering the dado in a hall with Art Nouveau style decoration.*

bearing wall. In others there were fretwork screens or panels of posts dividing off areas or a set of curtains at the bottom of the stairs to keep the upstairs private. In many houses it was still the area where visitors had to wait to meet a family member, so a seat and small table were provided, as well as perhaps a coat stand and small cast iron fireplace. Bell pulls beside the front door were connected by cables running in pipes to a doorbell or bell board, which can sometimes still be found. Telephones were relatively new at this date and seen as an upper class convenience, with a servant summoning the person who the call was intended for to the phone, which was usually rather utilitarian and often covered up by a domed case.

FIG 6.5: *In this large, central hall a small fold-down table was provided between the door from the kitchen (left) and that into the dining room (right) for servants to put down trays before entering.*

DINING ROOMS

In most large and medium sized houses, especially in conventional two room deep semis or terraces, the drawing room overlooked the garden at the rear, while the dining room was at the front. It was traditionally seen as a male orientated room and hence tended to have strong, masculine colours and decoration. A table and chairs were permanent features in the centre of the room so a dado rail was not essential to protect the wall (although they could be found for decoration in some cases). It was more usual to find just a picture rail (in fashionable houses it was in line with the tops of the doors) with a frieze above decorated with a relief or patterned wallpaper or stencilled.

In Arts and Crafts and Revivalist houses it was fashionable to have wood panelling covering the walls, usually around two-thirds of the way up, and often an exposed beamed ceiling, while Neo Georgian schemes featured shallow, moulded frames to create panels. Strong colours like reds and greens were used in both paint and patterned wallpaper (they made a suitable background for the pictures that were hung here) usually with a white or cream ceiling and cornice. In larger houses there would have been more than one room for eating, with some form

FIG 6.6: *An Edwardian dining room. Note the stencilled pattern above the picture rail, dark stained wood moulding and floorboards, the marble fire surround and the carver chair at the head of the table.*

FIG 6.7: *Although currently used as a lounge, the beam ceiling, dark wood fittings and its position next to the kitchen indicate that this was probably the original dining room in this Arts and Crafts style house.*

of back parlour (from the French verb 'parler' meaning to speak) for everyday family meals and conversations and a separate dining room reserved for entertaining.

Dark coloured polished hardwood tables and chairs were desirable although Arts and Crafts houses often had simple oak pieces, sometimes with rush-matted seats. The tabletop was usually plain as it was covered for meals and the chair where the man of the house sat was positioned at the head and would be a carver (with arms) to distinguish it from the rest. A quality fireplace in marble,

slate painted to simulate it, or a dark hardwood was preferable, otherwise an elaborate cast iron design or a softer wood with a dark paint or stain would have been fitted in this principal room. There would be a sideboard, often decorated or carved, with storage below and a top for serving food.

DRAWING ROOM
Shortened from 'withdrawing room', this was traditionally, as the name suggests, where the ladies withdrew after the meal while the gentlemen remained in the dining room, smoking and being

FIG 6.8: *An Edwardian drawing room. Note the French windows to the garden, display cabinet, fireplace with shelving for ornaments and the general lighter atmosphere compared with the dining room.*

thoroughly masculine! Hence the drawing room tended to reflect its feminine nature with a lighter decor and colours like pale blues and greens, rose pinks, lavender and soft creams. Rush and grass designs were popular both in wallpaper and as stencilled patterns upon the wall, the latter being a form of decoration that was frequently used in this room.

There would be simple groupings of seats, usually around small tables, as well as a piano, a grandfather clock and a bureau, along with cabinets to display the family's antiques, treasures and ornaments. The fireplace would be lighter in colour than in the dining room, often in wood with an overmantel featuring shelving and a mirror above. Despite the trend towards more spacious and simple interiors it was still easy for this room to become crammed full.

FIG 6.9: *An Arts and Crafts style drawing room fireplace with seating either side of the hearth, a glass display cabinet above the mantelpiece and shelving and drawers to each side (see also Fig 5.8, no 2).*

Medium to Small Houses

In the more modest house, the smaller semi and the masses of terraced houses, there were usually only two main rooms downstairs. Middle class households had always had the advantage of being able to separate their use and reserve one (usually the front room) for special occasions as a dining room or parlour, and the other as a living room (a term which first came into common use in this period). This was possible as they had a hallway up the side and service rooms at the rear. Now that many of the working classes had two up, two down accommodation they could copy their social superiors, and even though architects intended them to use both rooms for everyday living, the tenants often closed off the front for special occasions and Sunday lunch, and crammed themselves into the single rear room.

PARLOUR

In this best room, the family would fit a table and chairs with some form of dresser or cabinet to hold crockery and ornaments. If they could afford it a piano would have been squeezed in, probably providing the only form of home entertainment in this class of household. There would have been a stained wooden or cast iron fire surround with register grate, often with shallow shelving built

FIG 6.10: THE BLACK COUNTRY LIVING MUSEUM, DUDLEY, WEST MIDLANDS: *A restored front parlour (left) and rear living room (right) from a better quality two up, two down terrace.*

into the structure or fitted above the mantelpiece along with a mirror. A picture rail and a simple moulded cornice would have run around the top of the room with either a central or wall mounted gaslight in the best examples, and wallpaper covering the main body of the walls below.

REAR LIVING ROOM

In the medium sized terrace or semi where there was a separate kitchen and scullery to the side or in the rear extension, this room would have been used for everyday relaxing and meals. Comfortable chairs, a small table, storage and another fireplace would have been found. In an attempt to emulate the owners of larger houses, small corner bookcases or shelves and a writing desk or bureau may also have been fitted, in the fashion of the library and study of larger houses.

In smaller two up, two downs, however, this room doubled up as a kitchen so there would have been a small range cooker in place of the grate, along with a well scrubbed table, a small dresser or shelving and cupboards, and a sink bracketed off the wall. If there wasn't a separate scullery in a small rear extension or a separate block outside, the laundry rack and even the tin bath could have been stored here.

CHAPTER 7

Service Rooms

FIG 7.1: *An Edwardian kitchen from a large, detached property complete with a range set into the fireplace, a sink and drainer, a central table and built-in cupboards and drawers.*

The service area in a large Edwardian house had changed from that of fifty years before. The kitchen was now built into the body of the house and a smaller suite of rooms for preparation, storage and cleaning were either alongside or in an adjoining extension. This was partly due to the appearance of ready mixed and prepared foods, which reduced the need for the specialist rooms that would have been an important part of the older country houses where everything was produced on the estate. Another reason for building more service rooms within the main structure and improving their appearance was the general shortage of servants, which meant that better accommodation and conditions had to be provided to attract them and it was becoming acceptable for the lady of the house to become more involved behind the scenes.

It was the middle classes, however, who were most affected by the lack of staff (the total number of available servants remained the same – it was the explosion in middle class households that increased demand). In this class of house there could be two or three staff, including a cook and maid, down to a single live in servant, for all of whom life would have been lonely and their well being wholly dependent upon the relationship with the family. This was not a problem in the past when the only employment alternative was the farm or factory but now there were more appealing jobs in the new light industries and service sector and a life of servility controlled by bells was repulsive to many in the newly enfranchised working classes. The difficulty of employing servants had less effect on the upper classes at this stage as the large community of staff in their country houses and the higher status achieved by working there still provided an attractive proposition for aspiring butlers and maids.

The physical effect of these changes upon the middle class dwelling was to make the kitchen a major room within the structure of the house and encourage the introduction of labour saving devices and improved appliances. There was still clear separation between the family and staff, however – the door into the service rooms, which was often at the end of the hall beyond the stairs, would not only keep out cooking odours but also enforce this division in most households.

This was not an issue in smaller houses where the rear living room, by now usually with a separate scullery for the laundry, was used for preparation of food, cooking and eating. It is worth noting, though, that many working class families still spent little time at home. The man of the house laboured for many hours and often ate out; the women and older children might also work and it was still common for any cooking to be done in a bakehouse, usually beneath or at the rear of a local shop. The Sunday meal was one of the few times when they might all sit down together and had to prepare, cook and eat their food within the house.

KITCHEN

The Edwardian kitchen was not the multi-purpose, fashionably designed room it is today. It was rarely seen by guests and was used principally for cooking – not washing – hence decor was simple and light with an emphasis on hygiene. The room was only medium sized at best with separate adjoining spaces for the other tasks we perform in it these days. It was usually found in the body of the large or medium semi or detached house and in the rear extension of a similar sized terrace; however, in the smaller two up, two down the cooking usually took place in the rear living room (although it may have had the appearance of a kitchen).

The main feature in the kitchen was the range, a cast iron combination of oven, hotplates and boiler heated by a central fire and built into a recessed space with a chimney above. They had developed from simple open grates flanked by a boiler and oven in the late 18th century to more complex closed types by the end of the Victorian period. These typically had a roasting oven at one side of the enclosed fire and a baking oven at the other, with a hot water boiler built in above and to the rear, and hotplates with lift off rings on the upper surface. The heat for cooking was produced both directly from the fire and from the hot fumes, which were drawn around the apparatus by skilful control of dampers covering the flues. Closed ranges often had a removable

FIG 7.2: *A drawing showing some of the items that could be found in a larger Edwardian kitchen. (A) is the range, (B) a freestanding dresser, (C) the central table, and (D) the warming trolley. (E) is a portable roasting spit with a clockwork mechanism at the top, which rotated the joint hung below in front of the open part of the range.(F) is a rotary knife polisher, (G) a bain marie, which kept delicate sauces warm, (H) is a shelf for storage and (I) a gaslight.*

front panel so the fire could be open to heat a joint hanging within a portable roasting spit positioned in front of it as many cooks still preferred traditional roasting rather than cooking meat in the enclosed oven.

Ranges could vary from huge arrangements of ovens and hotplates, often with a separate open fire and spit, in the largest houses down to a compact form in working class terraces with just an oven and boiler (sometimes the latter was blanked off, especially in areas of hard water where they would quickly be rendered useless). The range, however, had many disadvantages. It was complicated to operate, which became a problem as skilled cooks became harder to employ; it was a nightmare to clean and required blackening on a regular basis; and many were horrendously inefficient with as little as 5% of the heat produced going into cooking, most being wasted in the room and up the chimney. The majority of ranges were still fuelled by coal, which meant that storage had to be close at hand for this, also a separate area for the ash it produced. There were few alternatives at this date although new, freestanding gas cookers were slowly improving and becoming more widespread but still had a reputation for being badly vented, dirty and leaving a taste of gas in the food!

In the middle of most kitchens there would have been a table for the preparation of food. Usually of a softwood like pine, it was regularly scrubbed with cleaning substances such as soda and sand (but not soap as this could taint food), a process which tended to leave the harder grain of the wood raised above the softer parts between. Architects and builders were more likely by this date to build in some form of storage, usually with drawers below a narrow top and cupboards above, although freestanding dressers with open shelves above and drawers, cupboards or a shelf below were sometimes fitted instead of this – or in addition. There would usually be a shallow sink and a

FIG 7.3: *A compact range from a rear living room of a two up, two down terrace house at the Black Country Living Museum in Dudley. Note the rotary spit mechanism suspended above the open part of the range for roasting meat.*

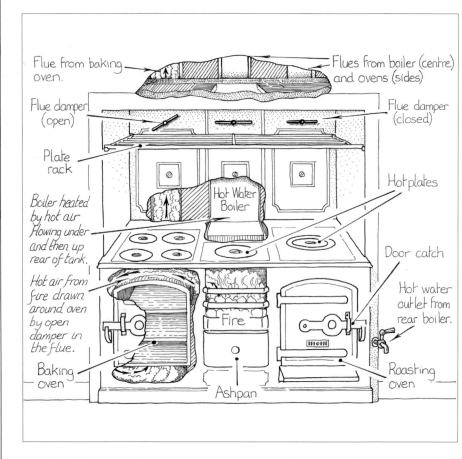

Flue from baking oven.

Flues from boiler (centre) and ovens (sides)

Flue damper (open)

Flue damper (closed)

Plate rack

Hotplates

Boiler heated by hot air flowing under and then up rear of tank.

Hot Water Boiler

Door catch

Hot air from fire drawn around oven by open damper in the flue.

Fire

Hot water outlet from rear boiler.

Baking oven

Roasting oven

Ashpan

FIG 7.4: *A diagram with cut away sections showing the parts and workings of a larger range cooker.*

tap, though these were for providing cold water and for use in the cooking process rather than for cleaning.

With hygiene the order of the day, the walls of most kitchens were covered at least halfway up with white glazed tiles and the remaining area whitewashed. Most had solid floors with red quarry tiles, perhaps with black border tiles, but some had floorboards as it cut down on

the noise made by scraping chairs if the cook and servants took their meals here (in the largest houses a separate servants' hall would have been provided). As people found it harder to find staff, especially in middle class households, the lady of the house was more likely to do the cooking and there was a growing market for cookery books and labour saving devices. The decoration might also

FIG 7.5: *A ceramic sink and wooden drainer of the type that could be found in the kitchen or scullery of a larger house.*

FIG 7.6: *A sink and hand pump from a scullery at the Black Country Living Museum. Note the set pot in the corner with the wooden lid covering the tank in which hot water was boiled from a fire beneath and ash cleared out from the hole in the base.*

be a bit more personal in this situation and not all would have been just sanitary white.

SCULLERY

The title of this room is derived from the Old French word 'escuele' meaning dish, and was traditionally the place adjacent to the kitchen where the crockery was washed. In larger houses messy food tasks like preparing meat, gutting fish and peeling vegetables were done here as well as the washing up after the meal. There would have been a table, sink, wooden drainers, a separate range or a hot water copper (a metal water tank heated by a fire below) and shelving. In this size of house there would usually be a separate laundry room, again with a range and/or a copper (the former used to heat irons as well as water), a mangle, typically with rubber rollers replacing the earlier wooden ones, a large table and drying racks suspended from the ceiling.

In medium and smaller houses the room was again next to the kitchen or rear living room, typically in the rear extension in a terrace where it was close to the water and drainage (often with the bathroom above for the same reason). It could be used for both washing up and laundry, with hot water provided by a small range, a separate set pot (a smaller copper, usually built into a corner within a brick surround casing) or from the main range in the kitchen, and cold water either from a mains tap or a hand pump. The sink was usually ceramic by this date and could be a shallow glazed earthenware or a deeper, white Belfast type, although metal lined wooden and stone sinks might still be found. The walls would have been whitewashed or painted a light blue, some better examples may have been partly tiled, while the floor was either flagged or covered in quarry tiles, often with a drain to take away any spilt water.

FIG 7.7: *A mangle and washing equipment from the days before washing machines. Clothes and linen were washed in these barrels or in sinks and dried by first using the mangle and then hanging out. The Edwardians were obsessed with whiteness so linen was washed in soda and lime or concentrate of potash or borax with Reckitts blue added to final rinse. It was then mangled, starched and ironed before being hung out on a line, or even on grass or hedge in a larger house, to bleach it in the sun. This was the period when the first mass produced cleaning brands began to become household names, especially as a result of advertising in the wide range of newspapers and magazines.*

In working class terraces of this date there would either be a scullery or wash house in the rear extension or as a separate block with basic washing facilities, a set pot and a sink, and in some cases this facility may have been shared with other households. In better examples the scullery was built into the house, leading off the rear living room where the cooking took place. In most situations this class of house rarely had a bathroom so a tin tub was located in most sculleries as this was where, usually, the only hot water was in the house. It would have been hung on a wall, hidden beneath a trap door in the floor or under a lift-up worktop, and pulled out and set up in front of the fire in here or the adjacent living room.

LARDERS AND THE PANTRY

Food storage was always a challenge in these days before fridges and freezers. In the largest houses there would have been

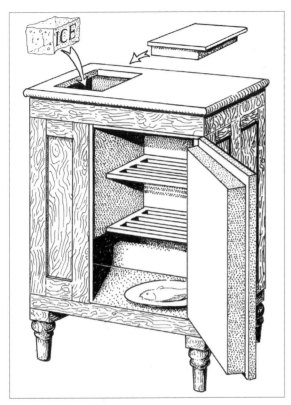

FIG 7.8: *A late Victorian ice box in which blocks of ice, supplied to the door by local merchants, were put in the chamber to the left to keep the perishables in the main body of the box cool.*

a number of separate areas for different produce. Larders (from Latin 'lardum' meaning bacon) could be found for storing meat, fish and general foodstuffs while pantries, which were originally where the bread was stored (the Latin for which is 'panis'), were also used for dairy products and some meats and were sometimes referred to as the dry larder.

There had been many improvements in the supply and storage of food over the past fifty years which helped it last longer and brought a wider range of products within reach of the middle and working classes. Tinned, pickled, preserved and dried foods became widely available

although there were also cases of dangerous chemicals being added to milk to increase its shelf life! The Agricultural Depression of the 1880s encouraged many farmers with good transport links to the towns and cities to convert their land to market gardening, and provide fresh fruit and vegetables to feed a growing urban demand. Meat was now cheaper as imports from around the world kept prices low, and fish, which formerly had been limited to coastal areas, was now widely available in towns and cities as the railways could speed the catch to the market the same day. This now meant that the middle classes could

FIG 7.9: *A larder with a low stone shelf and higher wooden ones, with a small, now glazed, window above.*

emulate the cuisine of their superiors and the working classes could have a more varied and better diet than their forefathers. As a result larders were provided in even the smallest houses.

The larder was usually a small room or a built-in cupboard positioned where possible on the cooler north or east side of the house. Walls that caught the sun might have an overhanging roof to cast shade or foliage grown up them to keep the temperature down! The room had to be vented, usually with a small window with gauze or a perforated metal sheet to keep flies out. Inside it had a tiled or flagged floor, hooks for meat in the ceiling and painted wooden shelving, while better examples had a cold stone surface at waist height for dairy products and setting jellies. Small larders like this tend to get in the way of later expansions of the kitchen and many have been knocked out, though their original location can often be found from the course of the original floor tiles or from the small window opening, if it has been retained, or on the outside, if it has been bricked up.

CHAPTER 8

Bedrooms and Bathrooms

FIG 8.1: *An Edwardian bedroom with a dressing table set within the bay window, a built-in cabinet with wash basin in the corner and a metal framed bed with a half tester (canopy) above.*

Bedrooms have not always been above the principal rooms of the house. In grand homes of the 17th and 18th century the owner would have slept in a room that was part of the ground floor public suite and received guests there (the king met his closest advisers in his cabinet, a small room adjoining his bedroom, and the name is still used for the ministers of state today). During the 19th century the bedroom retreated upstairs to become the private family area that it still is, with separate rooms for boys and girls. In the Edwardian house it was likely to share the first floor with a bathroom and separate water closet, a relatively new feature that had only become standard in large and medium houses in the final decades of Victoria's reign.

The upper floor in a smaller two up, two down terraced house would have simply had a couple of bedrooms, one for the parents the other for the children – any bathroom or toilet found today in this size of house will usually be a later addition. They would have been sparsely decorated, often with a number of children sharing a bed, and a chamber pot beneath to save a trek at night to the outside privy.

BEDROOMS

Bedrooms were generally lighter and less ornate spaces than the principal rooms downstairs, with hygiene just as important as decoration. Wallpaper in simple light floral, ribboned or striped patterns or plain painted walls, often in just white, were popular, some with a decorative frieze above the picture rail and a cornice, which could be coloured to match the fabrics. Floorboards were still dark stained, with removable carpets or rugs for ease of cleaning. Most bedrooms in all sizes of Edwardian houses had a fireplace, although many were only lit when someone was ill (not for just the heat but because it drew in fresh air, which was seen as healthy). Most were simple, compact designs, often in cast iron, with more elaborate types in wood usually only found in the main bedrooms.

The curtains in front facing rooms

FIG 8.2: *A modest bedroom from a terraced house with a small fireplace, dressing table and corner cabinet with a wash basin.*

would receive a similar treatment to those downstairs, with an outer blind, nets and the main curtains often under a pelmet, while side and rear facing rooms had more simple arrangements. The curtains tended to match all the other fabrics in the room, with muslin, light chintzes and lace being popular. In large houses the lady and gentleman of the house generally had separate bedrooms with interconnecting doors, while the main bedroom of more modest houses could have two singles or a double bed. These would either be metal framed or wooden bedsteads, some with ornate decoration and half testers (with a short canopy rather than a compete cover as on a four poster).

Built-in furniture was popular in fashionable interiors, often filling the alcoves either side of the fireplace and providing wardrobes and display space, although some Arts and Crafts designers preferred simple, freestanding pieces of furniture. Dressing tables with a mirror were usually sited in the bay or between two windows to get the best light, though in most large, and some medium sized, houses there would have been a separate, adjoining dressing room (these had been fitted in many older houses but had often been converted into bathrooms by this date). Other fittings might include a basin for washing (usually filled from a jug brought up by a servant), chairs or even a sofa, small tables, bedside cupboards and in some a bookcase.

BATHROOM

Edwardian bathrooms were much smaller than today's in respect of the space available, as most people still washed in

FIG 8.3: *Early bathrooms tended to have the bath and sink boxed-in using quality hardwoods (left), and although these can still be found in some Edwardian interiors most new bathrooms were stripped bare and were usually white in order to improve hygiene.*

FIG 8.4: *In the finest bathrooms a combination bath and shower, which could spray from all angles, was a prize feature. The taps in the right-hand view controlled (from top to bottom) the hot water, the spray, the cold water and the waste outlet.*

the bedroom. If larger ones are found, they are often a later conversion of a bedroom or expansion of the original. Most had only a bath, possibly with a shower in the best examples, a wash basin and some space for storage. Hot water was often provided by a gas-powered geyser, a freestanding or wall-mounted cylinder. Hygiene was top of the list when it came to design so unlike the mid Victorian bathrooms, which had all the fittings boarded in behind wooden panels, these were now open (Fig 8.3). The bath stood on legs, the wash basin on brackets and the walls were either tiled up to dado rail height or covered with a varnished paper. The room was predominantly white, although colours like blue were sometimes used. There may have also been pieces of furniture like a cabinet, chair or stool and some had decorative schemes, but generally even details like the pipes were left exposed in a room that was only used occasionally and not intended for public scrutiny.

FIG 8.5: *A marble surround complete with ceramic wash basin, brass taps and waste plunger.*

WATER CLOSET

Like the bathroom, the inside water closet was only a recent addition to the middle class dwelling. Most Victorians had either a flushing toilet in a small room adjoining the house or an earth closet (which released soil into the tank below to cover up the odours) in the yard or garden (the words 'toilet' and 'lavatory' only came into common use later in the 20th century and at this date still referred to dressing and washing). By the 1890s, with improvements in drainage and building regulations, most middle class houses had a small room upstairs, usually separate from the bathroom. The cistern would either have been mounted high up on cast iron brackets or might have been a quieter, lower positioned type, one of the more modern units that were becoming available. The room was small and bare but the basin could have a decorative pattern around the top and the seat could be made from a quality hardwood in the better examples. For the first time the new compact houses built for the working classes might have a water closet, although they were usually on the ground floor in a rear extension often accessible only from outside or at least separated by a small corridor. Some, however, still had an outside privy down the garden or at the back of the yard but at least building regulations stipulated that you didn't have to share with the neighbours any more!

FIG 8.6: *For most of the working classes a privy at the end of the garden or tucked in the corner of a yard with or without a water closet was often all they could expect.*

NURSERY

Another improvement in the late Victorian period was that more consideration was given to the children's environment. The sexes now had separate bedrooms and a nursery for play and education. In modest middle class households it was often squeezed into the attic while in larger houses it could be in the main body of the house. The room had to be the sunniest so faced south or as near to it as possible and – repeating the theme of hygiene – had easy clean flooring, usually linoleum or similar, with removable carpet or rugs on top. The fireplace would have been small and simple with some type of guard across it; a table and chairs was required for meals (children ate here, often only joining the family downstairs on Sundays); and a baby bath and cot would be kept here if there were any offspring that young.

CHAPTER 9

Gardens

FIG 9.1: *An Edwardian garden with rustic arch, terraces and a less formal planting scheme including mainly traditional indigenous species. As much care has been taken with the rear of the house as with the front so that the windows of the principal rooms have a clear view, with the service and storage rooms out of sight to the side.*

For a country obsessed with its gardens it is surprising that gardening became a widespread pastime at quite a late date. Although residents of even the most modest house had always spent time or money upon some form of interior decoration to improve their surroundings, few had the space, inclination or would lower themselves socially to do the same outside. The upper classes with their country estates had, of course, always been at the forefront of landscape design, and those less well off in rural locations had turned their plots to practical rather than decorative use. In the Georgian and early Victorian town house, however, gardens were less common; the rear of the large terraces was for the unpleasant services and not somewhere for leisure, a communal garden in a square at the front being the only greenery. Smaller urban houses had no such luxuries – a yard at the rear and the front facing directly onto the road provided no space for even a vegetable patch and allotments did not gain popularity until later in the century.

This changed, however, during the second half of the 19th century. With the lower price of land on the edge of town, gardens to the front and rear could be provided and, with the improvements in drains and flushing water closets, the back of the house was a more pleasant area to be in! For the middle classes, especially the lady of the house, gardening was becoming socially acceptable, and by the turn of the century the very structure of the house was being affected by its popularity. Edwardian semis and detached houses turned their orientation around and opened themselves to the garden with French windows, lean-to conservatories and terraces linking the interior to the outdoors, with the services discreetly masked by foliage to one side. Features such as bay windows and superior quality building materials, which previously would only adorn the outward face of the house, could now be found round the back on what could be called 'the garden front'. Even in smaller suburban terraces a garden was now common, although there was little scope for opening up the rear of the house on these narrower plots.

FIG 9.2: *A view showing how the rear of houses changed in the early part of the 20th century. The late Victorian terraced houses in the right foreground have rear extensions, which would have had the service rooms, water closet and coal stores, with no attempt to link them to the garden behind. The semis to the left, which date from some forty years later, however, have bow windows overlooking the garden now that the service rooms are within the main body of the house.*

REAR GARDENS

The garden at the rear of a large or medium sized house was more for leisure than practical use. Popular pastimes such as tea parties, croquet, tennis and gardening itself had to be catered for in any design, with more rudimentary features like vegetable patches and greenhouses relegated to the far end or hidden behind greenery or fencing. Terraces with cast iron or wooden furniture and edged with stone balustrades overlooked lawns, flowerbeds and the obligatory tennis court, the latter becoming such a fashionable accessory that it was squeezed into the most unsuitably small spaces. Paths tended to be straight with a surface of gravel, paving or tiles (in neutral or earthy colours). The boundary was marked by either vertical boarded fencing with caps upon the posts, tall hedges or, in some of the best examples, brick walls.

More fashionable gardens tried to break with this rather rigid geometry and reflected the motives of the Arts and Crafts movement by planting out indigenous species rather than the foreign ones that had been so popular in Victorian gardens. Sunflowers, poppies, roses, foxgloves and other traditional and fragrant flowers were used (hence freestanding glass conservatories required for exotic plants fell from favour). Rigid geometric plans were rejected for more naturalistic designs, with oak, elm, bamboo or rustic wood (with its bark left on) being used for furniture and garden features, and traditional details such as terracotta pots, topiary, box edging, trellises, pergolas and arbours were revived.

The medium sized or small garden would usually have a more rigid layout with a patio area nearest the house and a straight path, covered in cinders or beaten earth, down the middle of the lawn. Flowers and shrubs were laid out in borders around the edge or in a central bed and the property was usually bounded by a picket (pointed vertical stake) fence or privet hedge. In smaller terraced houses, where there was no time for leisure, the rear was a limited space for practical use with storage for coal and ash, washing lines, a privy and if you were lucky a vegetable patch.

FIG 9.3: BLACK COUNTRY LIVING MUSEUM, DUDLEY:
A small walled garden at the rear of a working class terrace.

FIG 9.4: *A selection of wooden gates of the type and style that could have been found in Edwardian gardens.*

FRONT GARDENS

A front garden was a sign of a better quality house and now in the more spacious suburbs even the smallest of terraced house would have a token space squeezed in between the pavement and façade. The area was usually left plain with a lawn or a hard covering, and the boundary was marked by a low brick or stone wall with either a wooden fence or metal railing on top of it (or a privet hedge behind). Picket fences and full height metal railings, usually cast iron although wrought iron came back into fashion, could also be found. Gates were either decorative metal types or wooden, with variations upon a design of a solid lower section and slatted upper being common. The Queen Anne style of white painted woodwork was still popular for the fences that ran on top of low walls, although on other houses dark colours including reds, greens, browns and black were used.

FIG 9.5: *Even at the front of terraces a small, token walled garden, which increased privacy and status, was usually inserted. Railings were originally set in the coping stones – but they would have been removed in the Second World War for munitions.*

FIG 9.6: *Black and white patterned ceramic tiles were popular in the porch and hall and even sometimes down the front path, as in these examples.*

Section III

Epilogue

End of an Era

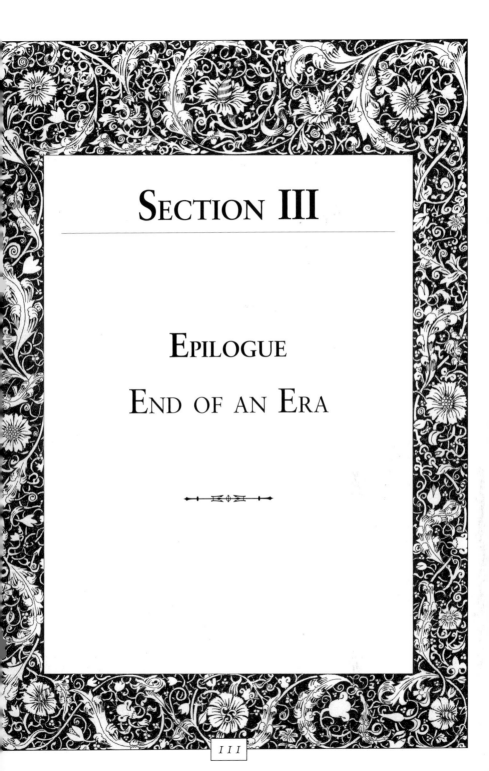

Epilogue
End of an Era

━━━ ✦ ━━━

The Great War: Prelude

From this distance it seems that the Great War brought a precise end to the halcyon days of Edwardian England, and its shocking catastrophe took by surprise the innocent thousands who cheerfully marched into its clutches. For the average Briton much of this was probably true. Although there was a deep underlying distrust of the Continent, few paid attention to international politics and modern warfare; there had been peace in Europe for some forty years and most people had greater awareness of events in far-flung corners of the Empire than of those just across the Channel. They were more concerned with domestic social issues, industrial unrest, the trouble in Ireland and the economy than with the squabbles of the European Powers. Yet international observers and those in authority presumed that a Great War was inevitable and all that was required was a spark to light the fire. The questions were only where and when.

The gathering storm centred around five great powers: Britain, Russia, the Austro-Hungarian Empire, France and Germany. The latter had been formed as recently as 1871 out of Prussia (which had just defeated the French) and a collection of Germanic kingdoms and principalities. Under Kaiser Wilhelm II, a great-nephew of Queen Victoria, it formed a Triple Alliance with the Austro-Hungarian Empire and Italy, and rapidly grew into a world-leading industrial and military power, viewed with both admiration and fear in neighbouring countries and Britain. In response, Russia and France formed a pact in 1894 and, although suspicious of both, Britain too aligned itself against Germany, partly through the efforts of Edward who had a personal dislike of his foreign relative.

The first place in which these gesturing powers came close to conflict was in Africa where they all had colonial interests and ambitions. The Boer War had been an embarrassing struggle for the British Army and left a bitter taste, especially as the Germans had been supplying the Boers with ammunition. To the north, the Kaiser provoked the French in Morocco when, after the Sultan had invited them in to help crush a local uprising in 1911, the German warship *Panther* was dispatched to ensure they did not stay! Diplomacy and combined threats from France and Britain diffused the situation, but just along the coast the Italians used the French presence in Morocco as a bargaining tool to permit their invasion of Libya, under the pretext that they were rescuing its own nationals from the oppression of the ruling Turks. This conflict against the once mighty Ottoman Turks was to have consequences in the Balkans – the spark that everyone had feared.

By the turn of the century this area, once part of the Ottoman Empire, encompassed a fragile framework of

FIG 10.1: THE CENOTAPH, WHITEHALL, LONDON: *This most recognisable of monuments to the Great War was designed by Sir Edwin Lutyens in 1919 (the word 'cenotaph' means 'an empty tomb' and came into common use only after the popular success of this work). For a few hours every year it becomes the centre of the nation's thoughts reflecting on this conflict and those since.*

countries despite complexities in their ethnic composition. The provinces of Bosnia and Hercegovina, although still nominally under the control of the Turks, was administered and garrisoned by Austria-Hungary, so when in 1908 a group known as the Young Turks took control of the old Empire, the Austro-Hungarians annexed the two provinces to ensure they did not revive ambitions there. The neighbouring Serbians, who had nationals within Bosnia and Hercegovina, cried foul and with Russian support threatened the alliance of Austria-Hungary and now Germany, and, although they stood down, the league of Balkan states they formed in the aftermath brought to an end the delicate status quo. So when the Turks became distracted by the Italian invasion of Libya, the Balkan League rose up and by 1913 had virtually pushed them out of Europe, with the Serbians becoming a dominant and confident force in the area.

The key event came on 28th June 1914 when Archduke Franz Ferdinand, heir to the Austro-Hungarian throne, was making an official visit to the Bosnian provincial capital of Sarajevo. On his way to the Town Hall a bomb was thrown at the car he and his wife were travelling in; fortunately it missed and did not explode, with the would-be assassin vanishing into the crowd. However, in a case of remarkable coincidence the Archduke's driver became lost later on the same day and stopped the car outside a café where the young Gavril Princip, the same man who hours before had thrown the bomb, was sitting. He could not believe his luck and made sure he did not miss a second time, shooting the couple before being bundled away by police. Austria-Hungary linked the assassination to Serbia and delivered an ultimatum, to which they replied by mobilising their forces. The pieces now fell into place as Russia lined up behind the Serbians and Germany behind the Austro-Hungarians. Britain at first kept its distance until realising that German domination of Europe would be bad for business; it then invoked an eighty year old treaty to protect Belgium's independence so, when the Kaiser's forces entered, war was declared.

At Home and Abroad 1914–1918

The fact that the Great Powers had been expecting this conflict is evident from the detailed plans for attack, which had long been in place and were immediately put into action upon declaration of war. The Germans had the problem of having to fight on both an Eastern and Western Front, but had assumed correctly that the French would be ready long before the Russians and so made their advance first into France. Despite counter moves and great losses on both sides in the opening months, the war on the Western Front ground to a stalemate, where it was largely to remain for the next three years even though there were periodic bombardments, incursions and retreats, which kept the casualty list high and morale low. The more complicated Eastern Front could boast gains measured in miles rather than feet but also lacked any decisive action until the Russians, crippled at home by industrial, agricultural and economic collapse, descended into revolution and withdrew from battle in March 1918. This allowed the Germans to release men to strengthen the Western Front where they had much success in the first half of that year. However, the arrival of the Americans en masse, more effective armoured tanks (to maintain secrecy they were said to be water tanks when they were first shipped around the country, hence the name), and the effects of the

Allies' blockade on morale at home, brought the war to a close, with the armistice signed on 11th November 1918.

The war years at home had begun with little initial effect, in fact the declaration of war on 4th August 1914 went unnoticed by many as it was a bank holiday! Britain's Army, although very professional and experienced, was small compared with Continental forces, but there was no shortage of volunteers signing up for glory on foreign fields. However, by 1915 problems were appearing, ammunition was low and the Government was slow to see the problem. It took the newspaper magnate Lord Northcliffe to highlight their shortcomings and encourage the opening of new factories, with many women filling the vacancies. Then the quality of those enlisting began to drop as recruiting sergeants found large proportions of working class men fit for nothing more than clerical work.

Houses continued to be built in the first year but in decreasing numbers and most work had ceased by 1916 as the full effect of war became apparent. Economies had to be made, with escalating inflation and the loss of hundreds of thousands of domestic servants who had left to get better pay in the factories or to fight on the Western Front. Although there was little direct action on these shores, apart from a few ineffective Zeppelin bombing raids, the U-boat sinking of merchant supply ships from America and the rest of the world began to bite at home, especially in 1917, whereupon rationing was introduced.

The Aftermath

One effect of the First World War is to blind us to the real developments that were taking place in the Edwardian period, as the years from 1901 to 1914 seem like the Indian summer of the Victorian world rather than the opening

FIG 10.2: *Despite the outbreak of war, some house building did continue, as with the case of this Neo Georgian terrace in Leek, Staffordshire, although by 1916 the full effects of the fighting brought nearly all projects to a stop.*

of the 20th century. It could be argued that many of the dramatic social, political and economic changes that would take place in its aftermath had their seeds in the decade before the war and may have occurred even if it had not broken out. Nevertheless the ending of hostilities saw many who had previously been complacent about social issues have to take action to deal with them – the Revolution in Russia the year before demonstrated what could happen if they did not. With regard to housing, it was at the top and bottom of the ladder that the greatest changes took place.

The upper class owners of country estates had faced numerous financial problems during the late Victorian and Edwardian periods. Rising taxes, death duties and the Agricultural Depression resulted in many being forced to sell off assets, town properties or – in the worst cases – their whole estate. Life was made even harder by the budget of 1909, further increases in taxes to meet the demand for new battleships and armaments, rent restrictions and, in 1919, the raising of death duties to 40%. Added to this, though, was the loss of male heirs in the conflict. One of the advantages of wealth is a good diet and young men from this background were not only the fittest recruits but also officer class, making them the first over the top when the shout came, and hence the first to fall when the bullets rained down. The result for the distressed family back home was all to often to sell up, or at least make do with what they had. The age of the country house had come to a end.

For the returning working class soldier there was more hope. The authorities now largely accepted that poor housing and living conditions were to blame for the unsuitability of many recruits from this social background, and under the banner of 'Homes Fit for Heroes' put subsidies in place so that local authorities could remove slums and erect new, healthier housing. Although legislation had existed before the war for this purpose, little had been done and municipal housing schemes were few, but now large scale council estates appeared in towns and cities, many of which were modelled on the structure and style of the houses that had appeared in the Edwardian garden suburbs. Some of these subsidies were also available for private builders, who still built the majority of homes, and the most recognisable face of inter-war housing is the masses of semis that line what were the new roads and estates in the rapidly expanding suburbs.

Summary
The Edwardian period was as much vibrant and inventive as it was retrospective and conservative. The world of Victorian self-sufficiency met the fledgling 20th century state support – early National Insurance, pensions, unemployment benefits and council housing schemes – head on. This clash was equally reflected in the houses built, as rigid blocks of small terraces were still being erected only a stone's throw from new, spacious and hygienic homes scattered along sinuous lanes and around mock village greens. There was great variety in the scale of the structures and also in style, with medieval, Tudor and Neo Georgian revivals competing with new interpretations of the past inspired by the Arts and Crafts movement. The Victorian terraces before and the inter-war semis after dominated their periods and can become monotonous in their repetition, whereas the clash of the old and new, large and small creates a rich diversity of forms that makes the Edwardian house a delight to discover and own.

SECTION IV

QUICK

REFERENCE

GUIDE

Dating Houses

Dating a house can be achieved visually or by using document-ation, the former method giving a quick but only approximate time-frame, the latter more time consuming but potentially more accurate. In most cases it will only be through the combination of a number of datable features and a selection of facts from various documents that the date of construction will be found. This task is much easier with respect to Edwardian houses as fashionable features can pin-point houses to this decade with more accuracy than is possible when dating older dwellings, and there are a greater number of records and maps available. You may also have access to the deeds, which should confirm when the house was first sold. If you do not, then the following sources may help.

Datestones: You may be fortunate enough to simply have a date emblazoned on the exterior of the house in question. These are usually in the form of a plaque, often with a house name, and were particularly common on middle class housing in the second half of the 19th century and the early 20th century. Be wary, though, of a few – especially on detailing such as gutters – as they may date an external makeover of an older house (although this is rare in the Edwardian period but often happened in the previous centuries).

Visual Dating: The photographs and drawings throughout this book, but especially those at the end of Chapter 4, may help to identify whether the house you are trying to date is from this period. Look at the pitch of the roof, the style of original windows and doors (including neighbouring properties), the bonding of the brick, the position of the chimney, the rear of the building and the form of detailing such as porches, arches and ornamentation. Although caution needs to be taken with older houses as fashions reached areas of the country at different times, improved travel, communication and the widespread availability of architectural magazines in the Edwardian period meant that new ideas could spread to distant parts in a matter of only a few years.

Documentary Evidence: There are numerous sources listed below, most of which are available from your local or county library or from the internet:

Maps: Ordnance Survey large scale maps were first published from 1888–93; the small scale (1 inch to a mile) first editions from 1805–73 could be inaccurate (republished by David and Charles); second series/editions were better, begun in the 1840s and complete by the end of the century. Be careful when interpreting the date of the map as there were revisions to add new railways and roads.

Trade directories: Listings of local businesses can be useful in dating when a street or row was in existence.

Victoria County Histories: A detailed series of books, which after a century is still only half complete! If your town or village is covered, you will find the description to be packed with useful information, and it often tells you when a road was laid out. Also look for The Buildings of England series by Nikolaus Pevsner, which covers each county and includes dating evidence on notable buildings in your town or village.

Other Sources: The census from 1841–1901 can be viewed at the Public Records Office (the 1901 census is also available via the internet). Also try tithe surveys (late 1830s) in the Public Records Office, plans for new roads and railways, fire insurance records, and local papers.

BIRMINGHAM BACK TO BACKS: Inge Street (next to Hippodrome Theatre), Birmingham, B5 4TE (telephone: 0121 666 7671, phone to book a visit as space is limited; website www.nationaltrust.org.uk). Restoration of four back to backs complete with interior fittings, laundry room and privies!

BLACK COUNTRY LIVING MUSEUM, Tipton Road, Dudley, West Midlands DY1 4SQ (telephone: 0121 557 9643; website: www.bclm.co.uk). Industrial village with authentic terraces, shops and chapel fitted out as they would have been in early 1900s. Very atmospheric with working features, and a must if you want to see how the majority of the population lived in this period.

BLACKWELL: THE ARTS AND CRAFTS HOUSE, Bowness-on-Windermere, Cumbria LA23 3JR (telephone: 015394 46139; website: www.blackwell.org.uk). Beautifully restored Arts and Crafts style house by Baillie Scott. Not only does it contain an ingenious hall and a startling drawing room but it is also blessed with views over the Lakes.

CASTLE DROGO, Drewsteignton, nr Exeter, Devon EX6 6PB (telephone: 01647 433306; website: www.nationaltrust.org.uk). A major country house built by Sir Edwin Lutyens and begun in 1911.

COGGES MANOR FARM MUSEUM, Church Lane, Cogges, Witney, Oxfordshire OX28 3LA (telephone: 01993 772602; website: www.cogges.org). Good example of a Victorian farmhouse kitchen with working range.

GEFFRYE MUSEUM, Kingsland Road, London E2 8EA (telephone: 0207 7739 9893; website: www.Geffrye-museum.org.uk). Period interiors on display.

NORTH OF ENGLAND OPEN AIR MUSEUM, Beamish, County Durham DA9 0RG (telephone: 0191 370 4000; website: www.beamish.org.uk). Exhibits fully fitted out houses and working features including trams.

STANDEN, West Hoathly Road, East Grinstead, West Sussex RH19 4NE (telephone: 01342 323029; website: www.nationaltrust.org.uk). Arts and Crafts house built in the 1890s by Philip Webb.

SUNNYCROFT, 200 Holyhead Road, Wellington, Telford, Shropshire TF1 2DF (telephone: 01952 242884; website: www.nationaltrust.org.uk). Late Victorian gentleman's suburban house.

VICTORIA AND ALBERT MUSEUM, Cromwell Road, London, SW7 2RL (telephone: 020 7942 2000; website: www.vam.ac.uk). Collections of period furniture and interior fittings.

The following estates are well worth an investigation as most are listed and many original features have been retained. However, the houses are not open to the public and owners' privacy should be respected.

BOURNVILLE, Selly Oak, Birmingham, West Midlands (websites: www.birminghamuk.com/bournville or www.bvt.org.uk (Bournville Village Trail) or www.cadbury.co.uk). Most early buildings of this still active housing scheme are centred around the triangular village green. Has the added benefit of being next to Cadbury's World!

HAMPSTEAD GARDEN SUBURB, North London (website: www.hgs.org.uk). In the area bounded by Finchley Road (A598) to the east and Falloden Way (A1) to the north. An exceptionally well preserved estate with the impressive central square and its two churches by Lutyens the highlight of a visit.

LETCHWORTH GARDEN CITY, Hertfordshire (website: www.letchworthgardencity.net/heritage). Most of the early building is in a ring around the centre with the Garden City Museum (Norton Way South) well worth a visit.

PORT SUNLIGHT, nr Birkenhead, The Wirral (website: www.portsunlight.org.uk). Splendid late Victorian and Edwardian Arts and Crafts style houses with much in original condition.

SALTAIRE, north of Bradford (shop and info: 01274 774993; website: www.thisisbradford.co.uk). Rigid grid pattern of stone terraces built in the 1850s–70s but an exceptional example of early housing schemes. Well worth a visit to see how far they had come when compared with Port Sunlight, for instance, built a few decades later.

GLOSSARY

AEDICULE:	The surrounding of a window or door by a raised moulding or pilasters with a form of pediment across the top. Common on classically styled houses from the 1830s.
ARCHITRAVE:	The lowest section of the entablature in classical architecture. In this context it refers to the door surround.
AREA:	Common name for the open space in front of a large terraced house down which steps led to the basement.
ASHLAR:	Smooth stone masonry with fine joints.
ASTYLER:	A façade with no vertical features such as columns.
BALUSTER:	Plain or decorated post supporting the stair rail.
BALUSTRADE:	A row of decorated uprights (balusters) with a rail along the top.
BARGEBOARD:	External vertical boards that protect the ends of the sloping roof on a gable and were often decorated.
BAY WINDOW:	A window projecting from the façade of a house, always resting on the ground even if rising up more than one storey.
BONDING:	The way bricks are laid in a wall with the different patterns formed by alternative arrangements of headers (the short ends) and stretchers (the long side).
BOW WINDOW:	A bay window with a curved plan.
CAPITAL:	The decorated top of a classical column.
CASEMENT:	A window that is hinged along the side.
CHIMNEYBREAST:	The main body of the chimney including the fireplace and flues.
CHIMNEYPIECE:	An internal fireplace surround.
COPING STONE:	A protective capping running along the top of a wall.
CORNICE:	The top section of the entablature, in this context referring to the moulding that runs around the top of an external or internal wall.
COVING:	A large concave moulding that covers the joint between the top of a wall and ceiling.
DADO:	The base of a classical column, but in this context referring to the bottom section of a wall between the skirting and chair (or dado) rail.
DORMER:	An upright window set in the angle of the roof and casting light into the attic rooms.

EAVES: The section of the roof timbers under the tiles or slates where they either meet the wall (and a parapet continues above) or project over it (usually protected by a fascia board which supports the guttering).

ENTABLATURE: The horizontal lintel supported by columns in a classical temple.

FAÇADE: The main vertical face of the house.

FANLIGHT: The window above a door lighting the hall beyond. Named after the radiating bars in semicircular Georgian and Regency versions.

FINIAL: An ornamental piece on top of a railing or the end of the roof ridge

FLUTING: The vertical concave grooves running up a column or pilaster.

FRIEZE: The middle section of the entablature, in this context referring to the section of the wall between the picture rail and cornice.

GABLE: The triangular upper section of wall at the end of a pitched roof. A Dutch or Flemish gable can be found in a variety of profiles, composed from geometric shapes.

GLAZING BARS: The internal divisions of a window that support the panes.

HEARTH: The stone or brick base of a fireplace.

INGLENOOK: A large recess providing room for seating beside a fireplace.

JAMBS: The vertical sides of an opening for a door or window.

KEYSTONE: The top stone in an arch, often projected as a feature.

LATH: A thin strip of wood pinned to vertical timbers in walls or the underside of joists on a ceiling to support the plaster. Also used on the exterior to help fix some renderings and hanging tiles

LINTEL: A flat beam that is fitted above a door or window to take the load of the wall above. In this period it was often masked on the outside by a shallow brick arch.

MOULDING: A decorative strip of wood, stone or plaster.

MULLION: A vertical member dividing a window.

ORIEL: A projecting window supported from the wall rather than the ground

PARAPET: The top section of wall, continuing above the sloping end of the roof.

PARGETING: A raised pattern formed from plaster on an external wall (popular originally in the east of England).

PEDIMENT: A low-pitched triangular feature supported by columns or pilasters above a classically styled door or window.

PILASTER: A flat classical column fixed to a wall or fireplace and projecting slightly from it.

PITCH: The angle by which a roof slopes. A plain sloping roof of two sides is called a pitched roof.

QUOIN: The corner stones at the junction of walls. Often raised above the surface, made from contrasting materials or finished differently from the rest of the wall for decorative effect.

RENDERING: A protective covering for a wall.

REVEAL: The sides (jambs) of a recessed window or door opening.

ROUGHCAST: A form of cement render containing small stones. Pebbledash is a variety of roughcast that has larger pebbles thrown at it before the last cement coat dries.

RUSTICATION: The cutting of stone or moulding of stucco into blocks separated by deep incised lines and sometimes with a rough-hewn finish. Often used to highlight the base of a classical styled house.

SASH WINDOW: A window of two separate sashes that slide vertically (or horizontally on smaller Yorkshire Sash windows).

SKIRTING: The protective strip of wood at the base of a wall.

STRING: The side support panel for a stair.

STRING COURSE: A horizontal band of bricks running across a façade and usually projecting.

STUCCO: A plaster that was used to render, imitate stonework and form decorative features, especially on classical styled houses.

TRACERY: The ribs that divide the top of a stone window and are formed into patterns.

TRANSOM: The horizontal bar in a window.

VERNACULAR: Buildings made from local materials in styles and method of construction passed down within a distinct area, as opposed to architect-designed structures made from mass produced materials.

VOUSSOIR: The wedged shaped stones or bricks that make up an arch.

BIBLIOGRAPHY

The following books may also be useful for further information:

Steven Adams *The Arts and Crafts Movement* (1987)
Isobelle Ariscombe *Arts and Crafts Style* (1991)
R.W. Brunskill *Brick Building in Britain* (1990)
R.W. Brunskill *Houses and Cottages of Britain* (1997)
G.D.H. Cole and Raymond Postgate *The Common People* 1746–1946 (1992)
Chris Cook and John Stevenson *The Longman Handbook of Modern British History* 1714–2001 (2001)
Jeremy Cooper *Victorian and Edwardian Furniture and Interiors* (1998)
Maria Costantino *Art Nouveau* (1999)
Mac Dowdy, Judith Miller and David Austin *Be Your Own House Detective* (1997)
David J. Eveleigh *Firegrates and Kitchen Ranges* (2000)
Juliet Gardiner *The Edwardian Country House* (2002)
Mark Girouard *Life in the English Country House* (1980)
Roy Hattersley *The Edwardians* (2004)
Charlotte Kelley *Arts and Crafts Sourcebook* (2001)
Richard Russell Lawrence and Teresa Chris *The Period House: Style, Detail and Decoration* 1774–1914 (1998)
Norman McCord *British History* 1815–1906 (1991)
Judith Miller *Period Fireplaces* (1996)
Judith Miller (and Jill Bace, David Rago, Suzanne Perrault) *Art Nouveau* (Dorling Kindersley 2004)
Nikolaus Pevsner *The Buildings of England* (various counties)
Tony Rivers, Dan Cruickshank, Gillian Darley and Martin Pawley *The Name of the Room* (1992)
Roy Strong *The Spirit of Britain* (2000)
Christopher Taylor *Village and Farmstead* (1983)
Adrian Tinniswood *Life in the English Country Cottage* (1995)
Pamela Todd *Arts and Crafts Companion* (2004)
David Watkin *English Architecture* (2001)
Kit Webb *The Victorian House* (*The Victorian Society Book of*) (2002)
Elizabeth Wilhide *Sir Edward Lutyens – Designing in the English Tradition* (2000)

Internet Sites:
www.birminghamuk.com/bournville
www.blackwell.org.uk
www.brentham.com
www.bricksandbrass.co.uk
www.british-history.ac.uk (Old Maps)
www.bvt.org.uk (Bournville Village Trail)
www.cadbury.co.uk
www.greatbuildings.com/architects
www.homeownersales.co.uk
www.hgs.org.uk (Hampstead Garden Suburb)
www.jrf.org.uk (Joseph Rowntree Foundation)
www.letchworthgardencity.net/heritage
www.liverpool.ndo.co.uk (Wavertree Estate)
www.lookingatbuildings.org.uk
www.portsunlight.org.uk
www.24hourmuseum.org.uk

INDEX